LARGER THAN LIFE

A HISTORY OF BOY BANDS FROM NKOTB TO BTS

MARIA SHERMAN

BLACK DOG
& LEVENTHAL
PUBLISHERS
NEW YORK

Black Dog & Leventhal Publishers
Hachette Book Group
1290 Avenue of the Americas
New York, NY 10104

www.hachettebookgroup.com
www.blackdogandleventhal.com

First Edition: July 2020

Black Dog & Leventhal Publishers is an imprint of Perseus Books, LLC, a subsidiary of Hachette Book Group, Inc. The Black Dog & Leventhal Publishers name and logo are trademarks of Hachette Book Group, Inc.

The publisher is not responsible for websites (or their content) that are not owned by the publisher.

The Hachette Speakers Bureau provides a wide range of authors for speaking events. To find out more, go to www.HachetteSpeakersBureau.com or call (866) 376-6591.

Print book interior design by Katie Benezra

Library of Congress Cataloging-in-Publication Data
Names: Sherman, Maria, author.
Title: Larger than life : a history of boy bands from NKOTB to BTS / Maria Sherman. Description:
First edition. | New York : Black Dog & Leventhal, 2020. |
    Includes index. | Summary: "Larger Than Life is a history of boy bands
    in popular music, from the 1990s to 2010s"— Provided by publisher.
Identifiers: LCCN 2019031819 | ISBN 9780762468911 (trade paperback) | ISBN
    9780762468904 (ebook)
Subjects: LCSH: Boy bands—History. | Popular music—History and criticism.
Classification: LCC ML3470 .S515 2020 | DDC 782.421640811—dc23
LC record available at https://lccn.loc.gov/2019031819

ISBNs: 978-0-7624-6891-1 (trade paperback), 978-0-7624-6890-4 (ebook)

Printed in Singapore

1010

10 9 8 7 6 5 4 3 2 1

DEDICATION

For Mom and Dad—

And anyone who has fallen in love with a boy band

CONTENTS

WHEN A GIRL LOVES A BOY BAND

I OFTEN JOKE, when someone is curious enough to ask when my love of boy bands started, that I don't remember life before One Direction. Nor do I care to.

(That last part isn't a bit. I really love One Direction.)

Sure, synapses fired as they always have, and my hearing has suffered from the impenetrable force of women and girls pulling from deep within their guts to contribute to the explosive, collective scream that follows boy bands wherever they may go, but that only feels like rebirth. There's no way to revisit a time before boy bands; that peculiar pop music virginity has vanished. When those floppy-haired English boys discordantly pranced into my life, I was a goner.

Finding 1D was exuberant, a feeling I assumed was inaccessible outside of adolescence or, like, falling in love. Because I was in my early twenties, both felt unobtainable and disappointing. Unlike the hip music I spent my days writing about in my nine-to-five as a music journalist (I still love that stuff and have the very disappointing tattoos to prove it), One Direction was in the market of joy. They never adhered to trends or to the canons set forth by vintage critics, the Recording Academy, and whichever Chad in Marketing secretly controls the algorithmic mood playlists on

streaming services. One Direction and the people who loved them loved them deeply, without fear of having their infatuation demonized as frivolous or feminine (two words often conflated, which this text is totally going to deconstruct). I was engrossed, surely to the point of journalistic biases, which quickly morphed into a mastery of a realm of pop music once ignored by my contemporaries. I wanted to write something that did justice to the modern boy band because, frankly, it's absurd that a book like the one you're holding didn't already exist.

If you've:

Ever been inconsolable with excitement at a live music event; **listened to a record on repeat;** thought people who dismiss Top 40 radio are elitist snobs; **been an elitist snob who changed their tune for some sexy ditty produced by Max Martin; traveled to another neighbor-hood, city, or country for the opportunity to see your boys in a different setting;** didn't tell your family about it; **handmade a band shirt or fan sign; destroyed a Trapper Keeper, notebook, or laptop case with stickers and scribbles for your favorite boy band;** read fan fiction; **written fan fiction; written fan fiction and later in life realized it was your first foray into a crucial, wholly embarrassing sexual awakening;** written diary entries, or blogs, or Twitter posts, or Instagram stories full of the same; **refused to leave your room, car, or any space where your favorite album was easily accessible; watched live performances on YouTube of your favorite group on repeat and lost hours doing so;** thought your parents didn't understand and knew your friends and other fans never could, not as much as you, anyhow; **wondered why your encyclopedic knowledge for music and evolutionary hairstyles is derided instead of celebrated the same way sports fans' menial fact-dropping is (which couldn't be as life-affirming, right?); have been genuinely afraid of how much you enjoyed a bit of music, a music video, or any other tangible aspect of boy band fandom, up to and including the sight of a plastic cup set ornamented with your favorite member's face in the discount bin of a Target, dollar store, or some overseas equivalent,**

this one's for you.

In the way that Judy Blume's books, Harry Potter, and other various young adult fiction turned a few generations of youths into voracious readers, boy bands continue to turn curious kids into curious music and pop culture experts. Boy bands teach morality, community, individuation, heartbreak, sex, virginity, purity, religion, politics, fashion, borders, language, business, dance, magic, nostalgia, and innocence. The affection inherent in these groups informs the rest of our lives. It's unsurprising that boy band fans past and present identify as enthusiasts, a unique name reserved for the likes of Anthony Bourdain and those of us unafraid to pursue the purity of pop, looking ridiculous and having a wonderful time soundtracked by silly anthems. And with that, let's get cooking.

BUT FIRST, THE DISCLAIMER: *Larger Than Life* is the story of boy bands, from New Edition through New Kids on the Block, Backstreet Boys, *NSYNC, the Jonas Brothers, One Direction, BTS, the great K-pop explosion, and more. While I'd like to think this text does a decent job of examining and fangirling over the best kind of popular music (that is inarguable—you have the book in your possession, so you know it is true), it would be impossible to cover every single boy band that has ever existed in one volume. Definitive histories don't exist, anyhow, and for that, I do apologize. What you have here is my very best attempt to include as many transformative groups as possible, without dilution or whitewashing or falling back on my own tastes. (Some biases are prevalent and unavoidable, and surprisingly, they don't all rhyme with Scharry Schyles.) If that's not good enough for you, well, I don't know, pal. Write your own book! Then send it to me, because that sounds rad as hell.

A Somehow Long, Definitely Very Abridged Boy Band Timeline

MID-1800s: An obsession with celebrity composer Franz Liszt is diagnosed as Lisztomania, one of the first modern, Western examples of pathologizing women's "hysteria" in relation to a musical artist. Girls are patronized for loving a cute musician boy as a collective disorder long before boy bands ruined our lives.

1930s: Barbershop quartets of men singing a cappella four-part harmonies emerge on the scene and grow in popularity. Lives = slightly more devastated. (Fact: African American quartets date much earlier, a tradition most commonly documented back to the mid-1800s. They sang spirituals but didn't evoke Liszt-level fanaticism. If I go too far back in the history of male vocal groups, I'll end up deciding any polyphonic singers, like eleventh-century Gregorian chanters, were the first boy bands, and I'd rather not sexualize monks. My abuela might read this.)

1940s–1950s: Following barbershop, post–World War II black youth, bored of their parents' music and dedicated to altering traditional harmony singing, create the love song craze of male doo-wop groups. It's swoon city, baby, population: all straight women.

1956: Frankie Lymon and the Teenagers release "Why Do Fools Fall in Love." Some fools fall in love with Frankie Lymon and the Teenagers.

1958: The Osmonds, a vest-and-blazer-sporting barbershop vocal group of Mormon siblings, form. Restorationism-practicing Christians deserve boy band hooks, too.

1959: Berry Gordy establishes Tamla Records in Detroit. In a few months, his company becomes Motown Records, Inc. His male vocal groups like the Temptations and the Four Tops become increasingly popular and increasingly proto-boy band.

1960: The Beatles form with John Lennon, Paul McCartney, George Harrison, and Stuart Sutcliffe. Ringo Starr doesn't join for another two years.

1965: In Gary, Indiana, the Jackson brothers become the Jackson 5. They will soon become one of the first boy bands and one of the first massively popular black acts to cross over to mainstream (read: white) audiences. Berry Gordy isn't sold on "kids groups" right away, but later changes his tune and signs them.

1966: The Beatles, riding high from their
success as the world's most popular
band (of boys), inspire the NBC sitcom
The Monkees, inadvertently creating the
first fully manufactured boy band. The
show ends two years later.

1970: The Beatles break up.

1970s: Scottish pop-rock boy band the Bay City Rollers inspire their
own Beatlemania called Rollermania, reaching the height of
popularity around 1974–1976.

1977: Puerto Rican boy band Menudo forms, ushering in a new
wave of Latin teen pop music.

1978: New Edition comes together in Boston, reaching the height
of popularity in the 1980s.

1984: New Kids on the Block are formed by Maurice Starr, the same
guy who discovered New Edition.

1985-1988: Boyz II Men, named after the New Edition song "Boys
to Men," get their start in Philadelphia, melting hearts with
R&B ballads and a cappella harmonies. To some, they're a
boy band. To others, they can't be, because they're too busy
performing seriously soulful new jack swing.
As *Billboard*'s Andrew Unterberger wrote of
the group, "Not all male vocal groups that
dress similarly can be boy bands."

1989: In Charlotte, North Carolina, two sets of brothers—Cedric "K-Ci" Hailey, Joel "JoJo" Hailey, Donald "DeVanté Swing" DeGrate, and Dalvin DeGrate—form Jodeci, a sexy, bad boy alternative to Boyz II Men's silky R&B.

1990: Take That makes their television debut on *The Hitman and Her* and launches the boy band revolution across the pond in the UK.

1992: Hanson forms five years before "MMMBop" would become inescapable. They work to repopularize the familial boy band format. In Seoul, Seo Taiji and Boys not only helped launch the rise of South Korean pop music, they become widely regarded as the first K-pop boy band, ever.

1993: In Ireland, Boyzone takes over the air waves. In Orlando, Lou Pearlman creates Backstreet Boys.

1994: Multiracial R&B boy band All-4-One blows up with "I Swear," a perfect medley of adult contemporary schmaltz and boy band inoffensiveness.

1995: Lou Pearlman creates *NSYNC to compete with the Backstreet Boys. A bunch of other boy bands come out of the woodwork to compete with one another, like 98 Degrees and LFO.

1996: New Edition reunites six years after disbanding and releases their first album in eight years, *Home Again*.

1997: Over in the UK, Five (styled 5ive) gears up for English domination.

1998: Producer Chris Stokes, recognizing a demand for more young black boy bands similar to the group that he managed in the early 1990s, Immature, introduces the world to B2K.

1999: Tween boy band Dream Street forms; they will break up after less than four years together. Frontman Jesse McCartney is a rare example of a soloist blowing up well beyond his midsize group.

2000: Like the Monkees before them, another fictional, caricatural boy band, 2Gether, is created for MTV's first-ever made-for-television movie. Unlike the Monkees, they are intentionally satirical. In the same year, O-Town comes together through MTV's (and Lou Pearlman's) reality TV experiment, *Making the Band*. In the UK, the line between boy band and pop-punk group blurs with the creation of Busted and, later, McFly.

2002: Both *NSYNC and Backstreet Boys embark on indefinite hiatuses.

2004: Justin Timberlake quits *NSYNC to go solo. Backstreet Boys return and get to work on their fourth studio LP, the aptly titled *Never Gone*. It drops in 2005.

2006: Big Bang, one of the biggest boy bands in K-pop history, finalizes their lineup. It will take a few years for them to explode in the West, but the seed has been planted.

2007: Disney, hot off the realization that actual bands— like, the guitar/bass/drums kind—are cool now, signs the Jonas Brothers.

2008: Mindless Behavior, an R&B boy band, rushes onto the scene. New Kids on the Block reunite for the first time in fourteen years.

2009: Big Time Rush, like a modern Monkees or a non-satirical 2Gether, forms because of a television show on Nickelodeon, a channel for kids. At the same time, the Wanted manifests through a series of mass auditions. Unfortunately, they're outshined by One Direction, but they have one big hit: the EDM-pop "Glad You Came."

2010: One Direction meets on *The X Factor UK* as soloists who are brought together by Svengali Simon Cowell. They will become the biggest boy band since the Backstreet Boys and *NSYNC.

2011: 5 Seconds of Summer, a group of pop-punkers from Sydney, Australia, form and quickly sign to Modest Management and One Direction LLC. That's right: they are a boy band at least partially owned by another boy band.

2012: UK boy band the Vamps are discovered on YouTube.

2013: BTS mobilizes in Seoul and changes the landscape of what a Korean boy band can do for a Western audience. *NSYNC reunites to perform at MTV's Video Music Awards, but it's a onetime thing. Australian YouTube comedy group the Janoskians go full-EDM boy band and release the biggest single of their career, the explicit "Best Friends."

2015: Brockhampton, a hip-hop musical collective from San Marcos, Texas, identifies as an "American boy band." Unlike traditional boy bands, they're celebrated by music media that otherwise doesn't cover teen pop music. They even score a television show with the cool, irreverent, and not at all kid-friendly Vice network.

2016: With One Direction recently disbanded, PrettyMuch and Why Don't We form and attempt to fill the boy band void while ushering in a new, contemporary look. Literally, they swap proper English polos for L.A. streetwear style.

2017: ABC launches *Boy Band*,
a reality TV show dedicated
to creating the next big boy
band. The victors start a
group called In Real Life. The
series is canceled after one
season. I don't know why. It
was great.

2019–2020: Following in the footsteps of New Kids on the Block
before them, the Jonas Brothers reunite, proving that in a teen
culture ruled by nostalgia, one life might not be enough.

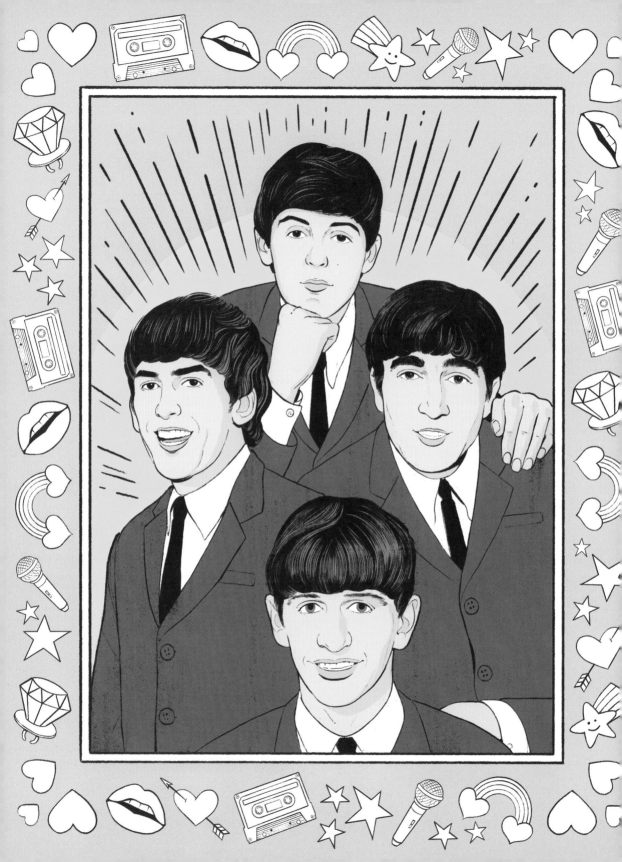

CHAPTER ONE

ON THE ORIGIN OF BOY BAND SPECIES

WHY DO FOOLS FALL IN LOVE: BOY BAND ANTIQUITY

MOST PEOPLE WITH a cursory understanding of boy bands will inform you that the phenomenon begins with the Beatles. If they're feeling boastful, they'll mention Beatlemania, a term coined in the early '60s to describe the absolute frenzy the coiffured foursome inspired within their female fan base. Those people, who I'm sure are super smart and cool and attractive and well meaning, could not be more wrong.

Like anything that's highly contested and old as hell, the origin of the boy band is not actually linear, but it is possible to get pretty close to a chronology. Personally, I believe the sensation that begat the melodious cutie-pie group was not the Beatles and their Beatlemania, but Franz Liszt and Lisztomania. In the mid-1800s, the Hungarian composer was essentially Justin Bieber; his very image was enough to make grown women faint to the floor. As Alan Walker wrote in his three-volume biography, *Franz Lizst: The Virtuoso Years, 1811–1847*, "Liszt once threw away an old cigar stump in the street under the watchful eyes of an infatuated lady-in-waiting, who reverently picked the offensive weed out of the gutter, had it encased in a locket and surrounded with the monogram 'F.L.' in diamonds, and went about her courtly duties unaware of the sickly odor it gave forth"—behavior strikingly similar to the monument erected in the spot on the side of Route 101 in Calabasas, California, where One Direction heartthrob Harry Styles threw up after a night of partying and a day of hiking in 2014. No wonder Beatlemania would share a suffix with Lisztomania a century later. If 1D came to fruition in a time when vintage misogyny was still hyped in pop-rock, it's likely "Directionmania" would've caught on.

But Liszt was one man, and boy bands require multiple members to fulfill meticulously crafted archetypes. Outside of the Christian religion, and its gospels and spirituals meant to venerate God, the secular male vocal groups that most resemble modern boy bands arrived in the form of barbershop quartets. In the 1930s, these were adult men who adorned uniform looks and sang exclusively a cappella. In the late 1940s, love-song-obsessed doo-wop, the result of black youth creating their own sound following World War II, transformed the group-of-dudes-singing blueprint with new rhythms and instruments. (Around this time, too, Frank Sinatra became the object of teen girl affection, a population referred to as "bobby soxers.") That music gave way to the popularization of rock and roll in the 1950s with artists like Chuck Berry and Little Richard. Elements of the hip-swinging genre date back to 1920s blues, but things really took off with rockabilly Elvis Presley, his female following itself very Lisztian, and other white artists who performed historically black music. Appropriation shapes much of pop culture, and it rears its ugly head in boy bands throughout the decades.

Elvis, of course, was also just one guy. You could argue that the boy band thing really kicked off in 1956, when multihyphenate rock-and-roll-rhythm-and-blues vocal group Frankie Lymon and the Teenagers released "Why Do Fools Fall in Love," a song so perfectly lovelorn it manages to masquerade its horniness, making it proto–every boy band, ever. How far off is "Love is a losing game / Love can be a shame / I know of a fool / You see / For that fool is me" from the Backstreet Boys' "Quit Playing Games (With My Heart)," really? And what a coincidence that Lymon wrote the song when he was thirteen years old, the same age Nick Carter was when he joined BSB.

The 1950s birthed superstars, but it did not create a group of equal members with boy band–branded ubiquity. Think about it: Bill Haley was the star of Bill Haley and His Comets, and they weren't called Nick Lachey and the 98 Degrees. Lymon and his guys arrived too early in history, as geniuses so often do, to be considered the first-ever boy band. That is in part because the decade marked one of the first real eras of the teenager, a postwar economic and generational divide that had never happened before. Young adults had money to spend on their own interests for the first time ever, and they would soon define popular taste.

With a chunk of change in their shallow pockets and iconoclastic impulses in tow, teenagers transformed everything in the '60s when the Beatles became widely recognized as the world's very first boy band (also the biggest pop group the world has ever seen, but whatever, those titles are one and the same; as soon as there were teens, there were teen girls hand-selecting what pop art was worthy of immortality). John Lennon, Paul McCartney, George Harrison, and Ringo Starr were a force, distinct personalities and talents that would go on to establish the modern boy band

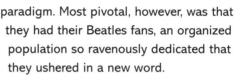

paradigm. Most pivotal, however, was that they had their Beatles fans, an organized population so ravenously dedicated that they ushered in a new word.

Beatlemania (a term that has been weaponized by the media to pathologize young women for going wild, screaming that decibel-shattering scream, and having a blast—imagine if anyone called male sports fans an "epidemic") marked the most vital shift of power in the boy band schema. The way the band has been described publicly is so intrinsically tied to their fans' ceaseless passion that they became one and the same, and Beatlemaniacs wielded their power freely. Their underwear-throwing, red-in-the-face, teary-eyed hollers for John, Paul, George, and Ringo were an extension of the 1960s sexual revolution, a real rebellion of gendered oppression, which journalists like *The New Statesman*'s Paul Johnson infamously misunderstood and thusly clocked as foolish, writing a deeply misogynistic screed: "Those who flock around the Beatles, who scream themselves into hysteria, whose vacant faces flicker over the TV screen, are the least fortunate of their generation, the dull, the idle, the failures." In retrospect, he was out of line, a real dolt, but the description does confirm two things: First, teens had taken control over pop culture, beginning in the 1960s and with the Beatles, as they would forever after. Second, boy band fans, specifically those who are women, were disparaged for their gusto, as they would be forever after.

GEORGE

The Beatles offered a framework that boy bands could build upon: John Lennon and Paul McCartney's unstoppable, joyful melodies (especially when dealing with love and not sex, at least, coded carnality in their early days) were at the heart of every song, as were their matching suits and mop-top bowl cuts. They broke records and produced hit after hit, without waning in quality and with exhaustive speed. They offered young people an image of autonomy that differed from other celebrity at the time. They were devilishly boyish. They were unafraid of meddling with traditional gender and genre structures; their music blended the blunt force of 1950s rock and roll with the outrageously addictive harmonies of girl groups like the Supremes. In fact, the Beatles worshipped those girl groups and aspired to be like them. What's more boy band–like than adoring women? The Beatles became extremely monetizable, their faces plastered on products and magazines and movies across the globe. Their influence was so immense that it would eventually create competition for themselves in the form of copycat acts. That, too, would prove to be a common thread throughout boy band history.

The Beatles' 1964 flick, *A Hard Day's Night*, made an impression on two wannabe filmmakers, Bob Rafelson and Bert Schneider, inspiring them to develop a series about four young lads in a global pop band. (Sound familiar? They were not subtle.) After a series of rejections, their concept sold to NBC, and their quartet, the Monkees, formed in 1966. The group was frequently referred to as the

RINGO

"Prefab Four," a parody of the Beatles' "Fab Four" nickname, and they enjoyed a five-year run, maintaining popularity even after their show was canceled in 1968. The comparisons didn't end there: the Monkees disbanded in 1971 (with reunions to follow), one year after the Beatles went their separate ways in 1970.

The 1960s were also the golden age of Berry Gordy's Motown, the Detroit-based Hitsville studio that produced hit single after hit single, combining soul, disco, R&B, and pop. As great critic Nelson George described it, Gordy created "a triumph and a contradiction...a testament to the power of black music." After a decade of timeless tunes and a path forged by the Four Tops and the Temptations, Motown's '70s were earmarked for boy band domination in the form of the Jackson 5. Even though Gordy's groups are rarely referred to as "boy bands" in the modern sense, the pieces were there: cute boys now with choreography, matching clothes, and seriously catchy hooks. Across the pond, Scotland attempted to release their own Beatles, the Bay City Rollers, and in Latin America, pulling from both Motown and the Beatles before them, Menudo became Puerto Rico's Monkees. Boy bands, long before the term was used, were diversifying.

At the end of the decade, in 1978, New Edition came into existence. The R&B group of youngsters, with the help of American producer Maurice Starr, became the first *contemporary* boy band, as they're described in popular culture today: they could dance, they were school age, they could harmonize, they sang love songs almost exclusively, and, as you'll soon find out, they were screwed over by a series of bad business decisions and the societal limitations placed on what a young black boy band was allowed to do in a racially charged US music industry. Though their songs pulled from Motown's crossover groups, New Edition was

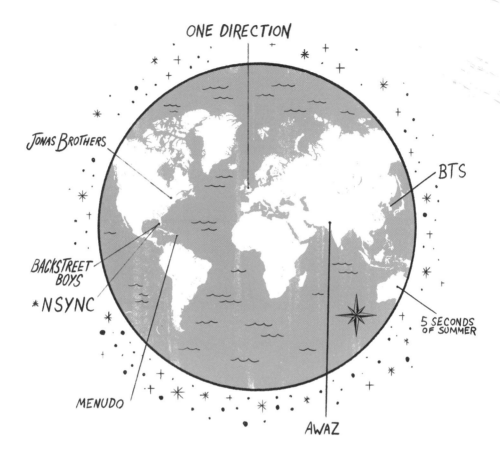

ONE DIRECTION

JONAS BROTHERS

BTS

BACKSTREET BOYS

*NSYNC

5 SECONDS OF SUMMER

MENUDO

AWAZ

labeled an urban act and therefore never fully commanded the mainstream market. Instead, some white boys from their hometown of Boston would reach the top—and with the help of Starr, the same producer who promised to make New Edition famous. They were called New Kids on the Block, and they quickly became '80s pop cultural markers on par with *Back to the Future*, the advent of the PG-13 film rating, and Cabbage Patch Kids. With their unparalleled success, boy bands were here to stay. And every generation would get their own.

CHAPTER TWO

BOY BAND 101

BOY BAND THEORY

WHAT IS A boy band? And who gets to decide which artists are worthy of the title? Surely a rose by any other name would smell as sweet? If you were clamoring for an expert definition here, you clearly haven't listened to many boy bands in your life. Don't worry. By the end of this, you'll be a pro.

Consider the most common interpretation. Merriam-Webster defines "boy band" as "a small ensemble of males in their teens or twenties who play pop songs geared especially to a young female audience," which is a fine line if you're trying to explain the attraction of K-pop to a baby boomer (my dad) without any real detail. A boy band is much more nuanced than that. A boy band is a juggernaut pop culture application whose impact is monolithic. Historically, yes, boy bands are hotties who harmonize, but fandom is the only true universal.

In truth, "boy band" means many different things to many different people; it's a living term that mutates with each passing generation, popular genre, socioeconomic shift, and, well, person talking about it. Yet, the majority of people seem to agree that boy bands adhere to some semblance of a formula (such as, a boy band is a group of cute boys who sing well together). For the most part, they embody those expectations. Except they also don't. There's a constant evolution and bending of archetypes every couple of years within the confines of boy band theory. That's the result of something called rebelliousness or, as my mother likes to refer to it, "annoying adolescence."

Still, in the teen pop lexicon, boy bands are defined by a set of characteristics worth unpacking. They are groups of attractive young men who dress similarly, dance without embarrassment, and sing well with one another. Each member fulfills a function: the bad boy, the heartthrob, the cute one, the big brother, and so on. They perform massive pop hits in stadiums full of teen girls coming into their own sense of self, in both their musical identities and their sexualities. They cultivate a space for total fanaticism with the help of expert marketing under the guidance of a single puppet master behind the scenes, pulling the strings. (I'll get to that later, but here's a short list to chew over in the meantime: the Beatles had Brian Epstein, the Bay City Rollers had Tam Paton, Menudo had Edgardo Díaz, New Edition and New Kids on the Block had Maurice Starr, Backstreet Boys and *NSYNC had Lou Pearlman, and One Direction had Simon Cowell.)

If there's anything to take from this crash course in boy band studies, it's that these groups play into stereotypes, but are not restricted to them, despite what the boy band hater in your life thinks. That guy sucks, but he's also the product of an environment that tells him boy bands don't have value. As you may have noticed by being a person in the world, boy bands are critically denigrated and culturally celebrated. They are written off as "uncool," an extension of a mainstream consensus that writes off what young women like as meritless and unworthy of conversation. It's the same misogynistic reason boy bands can have number 1 albums year after year, not to mention total ubiquity in stores around the globe and on the radio, yet still be panned, with no books written at an adult reading level about them. Because of their pop culture precarity, it's imperative to dissect the model to understand how boy bands are most commonly discussed and how they break the rules.

Hear that bell? School's in session.

THE ETYMOLOGY OF "BOY BAND"

Boy bands pre-date the widespread use of the term "boy band," which is only confusing if you're writing a history of boy bands. According to Backstreet Boys and *NSYNC impresario Lou Pearlman, the phrase is a few decades old and likely originated in 1980s Germany. "Years ago, the groups that were over there were actually bands playing music. Though they might have boys in them, they were bands because they played music. A group that would dance and sing was determined to be quoted a 'boy band,'" he told Frederick Levy, the author of 2000's pocket-size *The Ultimate Boy Band Book*. "It started back to the times of New Kids on the Block, and it also dates back to Take That. Once they had those bands, because they didn't play instruments per se, they called them boy bands, like boy toys. So, they're referring to a combination of boy toy, and they're a band, so they made it boy band."

Though no single person can officially claim coining the phrase (I'm sure some random guys do, and what an icebreaker to drop at the biergarten during Oktoberfest), there's a lot to unpack within the alliterative label. "Boy" is not "man." It's a gentler, playful, younger, less-developed gendered term. Adding "boy" softens "band," a word that replaced "guitar groups" in the early 1970s to separate rock bands (serious) from pop groups (frivolous). In doing so, "boy band" doesn't negate "band." The term actually combines all of its characteristics: a boy band features both musicians and non-musicians, instrumentalists and non-instrumentalists, as well as serious and frivolous elements. While "boy band" was created to describe and vilipend a type of popular music historically beloved by young women and disliked by older men, its origins* expose a much more complicated and interesting story.

THE BOYS

In Western pop music history, boy bands usually consist of three to five members, a legacy brought forth by Motown in groups like the Jackson 5, the Temptations, and the Four Tops. Adding more musicians runs the risk of overloading the fan base with too many facts to memorize: their parents' middle names, favorite colors, romantic endeavors, medical dossiers, and other paramount things of that nature. (In K-pop, however, groups can and regularly do explode into the double digits.)

The boys in a boy band are hand-selected by a producer, manager, or some other scheming businessman type who knows that the most successful groups require talent *and* unique personalities. If each guy occupies a role, the boy band as a whole can

---

* Boy bands themselves hate being called boy bands. As Lance Bass wrote in his 2007 memoir, *Out of Sync*, "To me, 'boy band' was a demeaning title because it took what we did and how we thought of ourselves—as a real group of performers who could sing in close harmony and move really well—and turned us by definition into something cheesy and assembly-line." In reality, his quote is a direct example of a musician internalizing the stigma and rejecting it. Which you could argue, and I will, proves my point.

appeal to a wide range of fans, as long as they remain completely nonthreatening to their young female fan base. And just like there are thrilling but predictable tropes in romantic comedies, boy bands thrive on clichés. They are the following.

THE HEARTTHROB

This hunk of man meat is often mistaken for the front man. In some ways, he is, but do not tell that to a boy band fan. This is meant to be a team effort. The heartthrob is most accurately identified as the playful, cheeky, outgoing, obscenely charming guy who is somehow always photographed in the middle of the group. Depending on his age and the stage of the band's career, he is most often shirtless. It's likely you're drawn to him by some inexplicable, universal force of libidal energy. Can charisma feel oppressive? It absolutely does when you glance at this guy. He is also the member most likely to have a super successful solo career post–boy band, shockingly based on more than his cheekbone to jawline ratio. He's got substance, sheeple, and his eyes are *up there,* not that you've been able to look away.

FAMOUS HEARTTHROBS IN BOY BAND HISTORY: 98 Degrees' Nick Lachey, *NSYNC's Justin Timberlake

THE BAD BOY

Everyone loves a rebel, and when you're a tween that means an unintimidating bad boy in a leather jacket. He looks dangerous, but he'd only cut class if you, girl, really wanted him to…and first period already leaked the news that Ms. Lockhart moved the chemistry pop quiz to next week, so you're good. He probably has the most creative haircut of the bunch (assuming the group is not totally uniform, à la the Beatles) and could very possibly have a

tattoo or several. He's attractive because he's an extrovert and undoubtedly confident. He looks like he could beat up the last guy who wronged you, but he definitely won't. He's a softie beneath all that unbreathable black fabric.

FAMOUS BAD BOYS IN BOY BAND HISTORY: 5 Seconds of Summer's Michael Clifford, New Kids on the Block's Donnie Wahlberg

THE CUTE ONE

Not to be mistaken for the heartthrob, the cute one is the baby of the group. He's probably the youngest member and, internally, might be known as the little brother of the band. In white boy bands, he's not always blond, but also yes, he is. Think of him as akin to Spider-Man. Compared to fellow superheroes Iron Man, Captain America, and Thor, he's super sweet and vigorously polite. He has been known to carry around a light cardigan on an early fall day in case the weather drops a few degrees in the evening. Unlike the bad boy, absolutely nothing about him is dangerous, which makes them the perfect

foil for each other. If he's in a group where some members have tattoos, his flesh is virginal. The youngest boy band fans have an affinity for him because he's similar to them in age and is extremely risk averse. Having a crush on him is as close to having a crush on a human teddy bear as you can get.

FAMOUS CUTIES IN BOY BAND HISTORY: Menudo's Ricky Martin, BTS's Jungkook (in Korean, the "cute one" is called the *maknae*)

THE RESPONSIBLE ONE

Sometimes referred to as "the older brother" or "the sensible one" of the group, the responsible member is the friend who orders a seltzer with lime at the bar to appear like he's drinking when he's not drinking. Practice is early tomorrow morning, and you bet your ass he's getting everyone out of there before midnight. He's likely the oldest member of the group, because maturity is supposed to come with age, duh. The responsible one shows boy band fans that, like a fine wine, men actually can get better with age.

FAMOUS BIG BROS IN BOY BAND HISTORY: The Jonas Brothers' Kevin Jonas, Hanson's Isaac Hanson

THE SHY ONE

This category is the most confounding because "shy" is actually a generous title. Others refer to this boy band role as "quiet," "mysterious," or God forbid, "the forgotten one." Because little is known about him compared to the others, the shy guy is intriguing to some fans; something about his meek mentality is attractive to those drawn to artistic introverts. Regrettably, "the shy one" is routinely a misnomer, a fifth category created to have five distinct tropes. At best, "shy" is a polite designation for an incredible vocalist with sharp facial features who lacks real idiosyncrasy. At worst, and most frequently, it's a racist demarcation used to describe the only person of color in an otherwise white group. There are exceptions to the rule, but they are exceptions.

As Jake Austen writes in his 2005 book *TV-a-Go-Go: Rock on TV from American Bandstand to American Idol*, the few nonwhite boy band and girl group members on singing competition shows, the ones from "Latin, Asian, Polynesian or mixed-race backgrounds," share "dark-haired, dark-eyed, relatively fair skinned looks that suggest ethnicity while still adhering to European standards of beauty…exotic yet not *too* ethnic." Basically, those who could pass as white, or whose appearance suggested whiteness, are allowed admittance to these groups, which makes the whole "mysterious" title even more damning.

FAMOUS SHY GUYS IN BOY BAND HISTORY:

The Backstreet Boys' Howie Dorough, One Direction's Zayn Malik

THE COMMANDMENTS

Apologies for the sacrilege, but if you're into boy bands, you've already converted into the most persuasive spiritual practice there is. Congratulations, by the way! It's a lifelong commitment, and it's much too late for you to back out now. The good thing is that there's no sacred scripture to memorize or eternal damnation to worry about, but there are commandments. You'll want to make sure you internalize this information to avoid appearing like a poser in future conversations. I don't make the rules, but boy band performers are forced to understand the following:

1. Thou shalt harmonize well with others
2. Thou shalt respect a five-year life span
3. Thou shalt not take the name of the fandom in vain
4. Remember your hair products, to keep them holy
5. Honor thy love ballads
6. Thou shalt not grow a beard
7. Thou shalt not get a girlfriend
8. Thou shalt be in thy teens or early twenties
9. Thou shalt consider choreography and coordinating outfits
10. Thou shalt not covet the limelight

Allow me to translate.

COMMANDMENT ONE: THOU SHALT HARMONIZE WELL WITH OTHERS

Boy bands must sing well together. Obviously. They don't play instruments, otherwise they would just be called a "band." Actually, some boy bands do play instruments. Much like organized religion, boy bands are full of contradictions. Learn to deal with it.

COMMANDMENT TWO: THOU SHALT RESPECT A FIVE-YEAR LIFE SPAN

Boy bands only last about five years, excluding, like, the Backstreet Boys and the inevitable reunion album or cruise. In the rare case a boy band exists beyond their expiration date, their popularity drops, and their celebrity is reserved for die-hard fans alone. Pop music trends have a short shelf life.

After the five-year mark, give or take, live shows move from stadiums to arenas to large clubs to small clubs and so on. It's rare for a boy band to elect to fade away instead of burning out with a fiery passion once they realize they've passed their prime and it's time to put this thing to bed. A new group is destined to take their place, anyway. As Boyzone and Westlife manager Louis Walsh wrote in the *Guardian* in 2001, "The rest is up to the girls. They go crazy, buy all their records, posters and DVDs and go to every show they can. And then they grow up. But the boys do, too; when you see facial hair, earrings and tattoos and they start to talk about being individuals, it's time to go to the conveyor belt and get a new set."

Even though boy band breakups are ineluctable, they are also ruthless and devastating for fans. When your fixation is happening in real time, it's impossible to imagine your favorite group choosing to do anything other than maintain their ongoing existence until you lose interest, as if you ever would.[*]

COMMANDMENT THREE: THOU SHALT NOT TAKE THE NAME OF THE FANDOM IN VAIN

Boy bands' only true loyalty is to their fans. Fans are all-powerful, and the boys know it.

COMMANDMENT FOUR: REMEMBER YOUR HAIR PRODUCTS, TO KEEP THEM HOLY

Boy bands have fantastic hair and work hard to ensure it always looks fantastic, even when dirty or disheveled, for their fans' sake.

COMMANDMENT FIVE: HONOR THY LOVE BALLADS

Boy bands *love* love ballads and would sing exclusively about the elusive four-letter word if they could. Many do. Sex, unsurprisingly, is not on the table, unless the topic is discussed through a heavy layer of lyrical metaphor and innuendo. Anything more is lewd.

COMMANDMENT SIX: THOU SHALT NOT GROW A BEARD

Boy bands are clean-shaven. Always. How else are you supposed to see those jawlines? Also, it's in the name: boy bands. Not "man bands." What kind of boy has a beard? Sometimes singers will sport light facial hair, but nothing more than a five o'clock shadow. The big beards arrive after the guys go solo, not unlike when a service member leaves the military and the war is over.

COMMANDMENT SEVEN: THOU SHALT NOT GET A GIRLFRIEND

The boys are unable to fall for any stone-cold fox until their fans have made it known that they'll remain supportive even if their

---

✱ There's an alternative mode of being, taken from my diary: you hope your band will stick with it until you get a cute boyfriend, even if it is some dude who thinks boy bands are wack. You decide to entertain his very bad opinions for, like, two years, because Mike is real, smells okay, and wants to do neck-kissing. (The next stage in the process is realizing boy bands are better than any boy you'll meet in grade school while simultaneously hoping your favorite group's reunion is nigh.)

crush is taken, or until their publicists have run the numbers and concluded that the boys would benefit from a high-profile relationship in the tabloids. Luckily enough, those realizations occur around the same time. Whether or not these extremely public bonds are real or fabricated is up to the fans to investigate, but it's very clear to see why, say, Justin Timberlake and Britney Spears would link up. They're hot, and the benefits are endless.

COMMANDMENT EIGHT: THOU SHALT BE IN THY TEENS OR EARLY TWENTIES

Boy band members are in their teens or twenties. They are never in their thirties, because then they might as well be dead. When they're in their thirties, they're officially men, which means they are not boys. Ideally, the youngest member and the oldest have

a significant age difference between them, too, to attract a broad range of fans. The youngest member is usually very young and therefore responsible for the oh-so-necessary falsetto. Someone has to hit those high notes.

COMMANDMENT NINE: THOU SHALT CONSIDER CHOREOGRAPHY AND COORDINATING OUTFITS

Boy bands dance. If they don't dance, they look good standing next to one another in coordinating outfits, which is almost as good as dancing.

COMMANDMENT TEN: THOU SHALT NOT COVET THE LIMELIGHT

Boy bands never allow one member to identity as the leader. When someone grows too big for his britches, the group is over. Got it? Good.

Over time, boy bands break free of their blueprint, the result of groups before them pushing the envelope enough for change to be had. Think about it: One Direction refused to dance a decade after the Backstreet Boys' and *NSYNC's massive popularity. 5 Seconds of Summer played instruments after them. K-pop boy bands like BTS extended the membership of boy bands to seven or more. Brockhampton raps, expanding the boy band genre designation from pop/rock/R&B to hip-hop. In future decades, these commandments may be completely obsolete, but one thing is eternal: cute boys who can sing well together will always be popular.

Or maybe a boy band can't be defined by a set of rules after all? Maybe a boy band is defined only by the makeup of its fans, the loyal young women who adore them? You decide.

LET'S TALK ABOUT (GIRLS') SEX(UALITY)

When cynics talk about boy bands, they usually paint a negative image of an uncritical, naïve audience. This is where the dark side of Beatlemania comes into play. Haters view boy bands as music for hysterical girls and self-infantilizing women with a partiality for losing their minds over a group of conventionally attractive young men, the kind who croon love songs with impeccable precision through perfectly crooked smiles, alluring accents, and cockeyed, floppy hair. In a shorter turn of phrase—and please read this in the style of *American Idol* judge Randy Jackson while disregarding that he absolutely did not say this and probably never would—it's "teens, predominantly those who love men, are hella horny" from me, dog.

There's nothing threatening about a girl in love with a boy band, but the way she's been written about suggests otherwise.

From "the dull, the idle, the failures" Beatles fan to the "butter-wouldn't-melt teenage girl" turned "rabid, knicker-wetting banshee who will tear off her own ears in hysterical fervour" One Direction fan (choice language from a British *GQ* critic who hopefully doesn't get any work anymore), fangirls are described as ceaselessly aroused toxic creatures from the black lagoon instead of the pop culture aficionados they actually are. Someone should let him know that female fandom doesn't exist on the fringe of and for men's experience.

One thing the chauvinists fail to recognize or respect, in a laundry list of things they fail to recognize or respect, is the baseline self-determinism that liking a boy band introduces within its predominantly female audience. For many, these groups kick-start a sexual awakening, sure. *Do I like boys? What kind of boys do I like?* Or *Do I want to be these men? Do I have no interest in touching parts with them whatsoever? Do I relate most to the queer member because I, myself, might be gay?* Female sexuality has never been praised; it certainly has never been given a place to commune in tweendom. Boy bands allow straight women and girls to not only relish in their own lustfulness but also, in the live concert setting, share their passion with their fellow sisters, to scream it, even if they're not yet sure why those boys have elicited such a strong reaction from within them.

BOY BAND MASCULINITY ON THE MARGINS, ANDROGYNY, AND A NEW KIND OF SEX SYMBOL

Here's a short list of various goods and services *Cosmopolitan* has rated "things men think are manly": beards, big dogs, cars, guns, steaks, fighting, football, lumberjacking (the world's second oldest profession?), explosions, leather jackets, whiskey, cigars, man caves, and not asking for directions. All of the objects are shit brown in color, and none of the concepts will come up in a word-association game where the prompt is "boy band." "Cars" might come close, but BTS's school bus in the "No More Dream" music video or the sexy turquoise convertible in New Edition's "If It Isn't Love" would be more accurate. This is a long-winded way of introducing the dangerous concept of manliness as a social construct. All of the aforementioned antiquated notions of brute-strength dude stuff gets thrown out of the window when discussing boy bands, and everyone is the better for it.

As the record has established, boy bands exist on the margins of pop culture and its coverage. Unsurprisingly, their dominant fandom reflects those margins. I'm speaking of the minority groups who love and adore them, young women and gay men and other populations who rarely get their fair share—a nasty effect of boy bands being big business, and big business thriving on binaries where whole demographics are depressed into marketable bars on a graph. However, boy bands' expressions of masculinity, too, exist on the dynamic margins, which makes their "manhood" fertile ground for investigation, the same way critics have long inter-rogated David Bowie's queer aesthetics, or '80s Goth bands that generously layered their lashes with mascara (that one is for the Robert Smith fans in the room), or Jaden Smith's and Young Thug's fashionable hip-hop androgyny. It's no wonder that in recent years, boy bands have become the focus of some ethnomusicological study as purveyors of a new kind of gender neutrality: soft, chaste, and borderline fluid.

> **ATTENTION!** I'm interrupting the regularly scheduled programming to bring you an academic message. This will be worthwhile. Maybe one day when you're on a blind date and your match says something stupid like, "I don't get why 5 Seconds of Summer were such a big deal," you can school them in a few succinct paragraphs. Make sure to elongate these points with your own personal flair just enough to get a full meal out of the deal, then promptly leave the restaurant because they aren't for you and you're never going to see that jerk again. **Please stand by.**

In the article "Marketing Androgyny: The Evolution of the Backstreet Boys," scholar Daryl Jamieson describes a trend in popular culture as a move "away from idealizing mature, strong 'men' in favor of young, androgynous 'boys.'" Think Nick Carter as the ultimate dreamboat instead of Humphrey Bogart or, like, Dwayne "The Rock" Johnson. He writes, "The reasons for this generational reversal in tastes among straight females are no doubt many, varied, and complex…pop music, if not the prime instigator of this trend, has played a major role in perpetuating it, and introducing it to each new generation of consumers. And one of the principal vehicles for this cultural shift is the manufactured band." This trend, he claims, has developed a "relatively new type of male sex symbol…sensitive…soft-skinned, usually blonde, thin (if not emaciated), youthful (which implies a lack of body and facial hair, boundless energy, as well as a certain coy naivete), fashionable and possesses an above-average ability to dance; he is, in a word, androgynous, embodying in roughly equal proportions traits which are traditionally perceived as masculine and feminine." Those are not words associated with a vintage hardened machismo.

Instead of hiding behind the mysterious rock god banality of 1970s celebrities before them, boy bands are transparent in their wants, needs, and desires (or, better put, transparent in the way their marketing strategies are articulated to us). They are radically earnest with their feelings, not something that accompanies conversations of Western virility as much as, say, beer and sports might. Boy bands intentionally renounce symbols of toxic masculinity, too: as academic Georgina Gregory points out in her book *Boy Bands and the Performance of Pop Masculinity*, in One Direction's 2011 song "Save You Tonight," the guys sing, "I can't be no superman / But for you I'll be superhuman." Strength, and the strength of their adoration, is explicitly not-male.

Gregory argues (and I'm obviously paraphrasing here) that in the pop space, being a hottie is a requirement for both men and women. Rock star guys don't need to be conventionally attractive. (Any motivated, unfortunate-faced person can learn to shred a six string. Go to a Guitar Center and you'll see what I mean, and I say that as a previously motivated, unfortunate-faced person who once loved a gratuitous solo.) Boy bands use their good looks to their advantage, but handsomeness is also a necessity for them. They share a lot of the same requirements of women performers, too, the most obvious happen to be an attractive appearance* viewed by naysayers as a stand-in for virtuosity, and a heavy dose of empathy as cultural currency.

There's a whole book to be written about the politics of positioning these boys outside of the male gaze, the feminist theory that women in art and history are portrayed by men as submissive, sexual objects. Gregory points out that by performing on a stage, boy bands are looked at and objectified, similar to how women are in everyday life. (Of course, those men are also compensated in the process, whereas women live in danger of abuse, fear of harm, and perennial subjugation by the men whose hungry eyes feast upon them. Boy bands don't walk alone at night with keys between their fingers like some makeshift Wolverine to protect themselves from evil.) Nevertheless, it goes without question that boy bands subvert harmful, traditional images of what a man is supposed to be and offer an inviting alternative. They dare to exist not to uphold straight cis men's interest, but to celebrate marginalized people's humanity. That's pretty cool. Dare I say…manly, even?

✻ Physical size isn't discussed enough. Boy band members are expected to have slender or athletic builds and that's it. Those are the options. They're never too muscular, because that gives the appearance of old-school macho men, but they may choose to bulk up later in life. Few have drifted from the status quo, and there has never been an ultra-famous fat boy band singer. The best example of someone challenging the norm is probably Take That's Gary Barlow. His weight fluctuated more than other boys in bands, to the extent that when Take That released dolls of its members, Gregory writes, his was given away for free as an incentive for consumers to buy the others. Someone, apparently, was under the impression that Thatters couldn't love a chubby icon. If that's not bad enough, Simon Cowell once said, "I'll sign them, without the fat one," about the band, which he has since come to regret. Free idea for any music-manager hopefuls reading this: there has yet to be a fat-acceptance boy band movement, and I'm ready.

A Short List of Absolutely Crucial Boy Band Lingo

TO FULLY DIVE into the boy band story, there are some terms to familiarize yourself with in order to make it through the overwhelming enthusiasm of it all. I'm very much aware that slang limits text to an isolated moment in time, but this is a history book (a tongue-in-cheek history, but a social study nonetheless) that requires you, dear reader, to wield the proper tools to make it through. Luckily enough, you're armed.

"THE BOYS": This is how all boy band fans refer to their favorite group. If they're feeling assertive, it becomes "my boys." When communicating with another die-hard devotee, it's "our boys."

EASTER EGG: In popular culture, an Easter egg is a hidden message, joke, reference, or image in a body of work meant for fans to decode or crack. For example, New Kids on the Block wearing updated versions of their "Hanging Tough" outfits in the video for their "Boys in the Band" single thirty years after the original track is an Easter egg. It's unlikely a non-NKOTB fan would pick up on it.

FAN FICTION (FAN FIC FOR SHORT): This one is pretty self-explanatory, but fan fiction is fiction based on real people or characters from a separate, original work. There can be Harry Potter fan fiction, and there can be fan fic about befriending New Kids on the Block. If they so happen to travel to space and land on a planet that does not exist in our limited understanding of the great beyond, or enter some other setting that differs from their canonical history, that's referred to as AU, or fan fiction set in "alternative universes." Online, there are self-publishing databases dedicated to fan fiction, the largest one being Wattpad. You might remember Fanfiction.net.

FANDOM (AND FANDOM NAME): Fandom is used to describe both a community of fans and the experience of being a fan. Etymologically, it is the combination of fan- and the suffix -dom, likely referring to "kingdom," or a condition, found in the word "wisdom." In the latter interpretation, "fandom" is the state of being a fan. Every big boy band, and those groups who aspire to one day become a big boy band, name their fandoms. It's a simple idea: give your loyal followers a sense of community and identity by tagging them in the same way Democratic and Republican party affiliations unite people with similar politics. Contrary to popular belief, fandom names are not a trend that began in the social media age to rally those populations. They have been around for decades: the Beatles had their Beatlemaniacs, the Bay City Rollers had Rollermaniacs, New Kids on the Block fans are called Blockheads, Direction has its Directioners, BTS simply calls their group ARMY, like KISS fans referred to themselves in the zenith of '80s hair metal.

FAVE(S): Your favorite band, bands, member, celebrities, whatever. It is not a proper noun, but the internet does not care much for grammar or the limitations of language, so get used to it. Example: Big Bang's G-Dragon is my fave.

INSIDER: A term used to describe the most loyal and active members of an online fan account who have access to privileged information, like the whereabouts of a boy band beyond their publicized appearances. These include: the hotels they're staying at, where they were spotted in the last hour, their flight numbers, and so on. This should not be confused with the way "insider" is used at gossip publications, where it means a private source close to a celebrity. These insiders are fans who've done their homework and should probably become spies later in life.

SHIP: While this may sound nautical to the uninitiated, "ship" is closer to "relationship" than "pirate ship." It's an active verb. When a fan ships, they encourage and/or root for a relationship between two celebs and/or fictional characters. This is anything from hoping Harry Potter and Hermione Granger would become an item to wishing boy band members would date one another. Shipping plays a crucial role in celebrity gossip and in the homosocial experiences of fans who, say, want One Direction's Harry Styles and Louis Tomlinson to date. In fact, romantically positioning two objects of affection in queer relationships is common in boy band spaces. For many young women interested in the boys, it would be heartbreaking to see them with another girl, but with another member of the group—someone she also fancies—it's accessible eroticism. In that way, shipping deserves a lot of thought: Is it that these girls see queer relationships as somehow less legitimate than straight ones, and therefore this does nothing toward furthering sexual equality? That Harry and Louis together means they could never "cheat" on a female fan? Or is it that fans are open to the idea of polyamory and bi/pansexual identity at an early age? Or are they simply horny?

SHIP NAME: When you ship a pair, it's likely that others do, too. That results in a sub-fandom for those relationships, regardless of whether or not they are real. To return to the previous example: Harry Styles and Louis Tomlinson shippers are known as Larries, in reference to "Larry Stylinson," a combination of both boys' names. When Styles was dating Taylor Swift, a public relationship, their ship name was "Haylor."

STALK: Not to be confused with the criminal act of harassing someone with unwanted obsession, "stalking" is used by boy band fans in a way that is meant to reappropriate the "hysterical" language of boy band fandom past. A stan "stalks" by waiting around a place their fave member might be, such as outside a tour bus following a stadium set or at baggage claim in an airport. A fan could say they're "stalking" their fave by simply scrolling through social media and bringing attention to some posts he recently liked. Basically, stalking ranges from the totally innocuous to borderline criminal.

STAN: A portmanteau of "stalker" and "fan," colloquially used to mean "super fan." Taken from a 2000 Eminem song no one should remember. Or perhaps they should, for the horror. In the lyrics, "Stan" is an obsessed fan who gets drunk and drives off a cliff with his pregnant girlfriend in the trunk, presumably because Eminem, his obsession, never responded to his fan letters. Nowadays, the term has been co-opted by fan culture and used endearingly, both as a noun ("I'm an O-Town stan") and a verb ("She stans New Edition").

TINHATTING: Taken from the conspiratorial impulse to rock a tinfoil hat, à la the 2002 flick *Signs*, tinhatting is the fan practice of forming some theory and using new information to justify it. In my profession, that's called lazy journalism: the result of someone who has already come to a conclusion looking for and stretching shreds of evidence to verify their existing thesis instead of allowing an unbiased investigation to uncover the truth. But it can be fun to be obnoxious online, in zines, and with friends, so more power to the tinhatters—as long as they aren't promoting harm.

CHAPTER THREE

HANGIN' TOUGH: NEW KIDS ON THE BLOCK

FROM MOTOWN TO MENUDO: BLACK AND BROWN PEOPLE INVENTED THE MODERN BOY BAND

AS PREVIOUSLY ALLUDED, the modern boy band—defined as a group of young men singing melodiously and dancing together— did not begin in the '80s when Boston brats New Kids on the Block stormed onto boom boxes and Walkmen everywhere, hangin' tough. In the midst of the '60s and '70s, the Beatles' desire to hold some hands, the Bay City Rollers' jeers for S-A-T-U-R-D-A-Y night, and a celebration of African American music like R&B and soul in the mainstream by a white teenage generation more tolerant than their parents, a new era of boy bands was being built. And contrary to the contemporary image of these harmo- nizing hunks, they were people of color.

For example: Motown Records.

Mic drop.

Next question.

I'm kidding, except, uh, not at all. Motown not only proved that white audiences would listen to, love, and collaborate with black artists, the label also brought forth black vocal groups like the Jackson 5, the Four Tops, and the Temptations, whose infusion of R&B, soul, gospel, jazz, rock and roll, and pop delighted audiences nationwide beyond groups of young women. On paper, much of what these Motown groups did screamed "boy band" and, had the term existed at the time, they probably would've been branded that way by the press. Instead, they're viewed as artists with a swoon-worthy energy that registers more like straight-up romance than youthful crushing. They performed hits still beloved today—such as "I Can't Help Myself (Sugar Pie Honey Bunch)" by the Four Tops and "My Girl" by the Temptations—and they did so by abiding by Motown creator Berry Gordy's opaque factory system, the very same that boy band masterminds would imitate in the '80s, '90s, '00s, and beyond.

Gordy, formerly an assembly line worker at Ford's factory in Detroit, where his famed Hitsville U.S.A., home of Motown Records, was headquartered, took what he learned in the warehouse and applied it to the music business. He ran a tight ship that included morning writing and recording sessions and a rotating cast and crew of various talents who'd try the same song countless times with different arrangements until they reached perfection. Once the song did, he found a way to replicate the process, production line style, and quick. In automotive terms, he instituted quality control and mass manufacturing. To Gordy, something as subjective as music could be streamlined, even conquered. Long hours and a tireless work schedule made his shop one full of master craftsmen, the same thoroughgoing, high-risk, high-reward practice that links all boy bands to one another. There's no rest for the ambitious.

Latin America, too, had already been bitten by the boy band bug before the music overwhelmed US audiences with New Kids on the Block. In 1977, producer Edgardo Díaz formed Menudo in San Juan, Puerto Rico, the largest group the island had ever seen and one of the most successful Latin groups in music history. Disregarding the five-year rule, Menudo's first run lasted two decades because of the unusual way the boy band was set up. Members were replaced once they turned sixteen—a seemingly cutthroat business practice. (A few beloved boys got to remain in the band a bit longer, but only superstars like Ricky Martin and Draco Rosa. Most did not.) By keeping his boys forever young, by keeping them *boys*, Díaz ensured that their voices would never descend too low with the effects of puberty, and that Menudo would maintain an equally

young, perennially replenishing audience. For that reason, their music has always been child-friendly, but over time, their look moved from sneakers to skinny jeans and a bit sexier clothing, a brilliant play for the loyal young women in the crowd.

Unlike the Motown model, a business engine that aimed to release the best possible songs, Menudo styled themselves with the manufactured gloss of the Monkees, just without a Beatles-like band to impersonate—a business engine that aimed to sell product. Menudo's mass-marketed, lip-synced music was recorded in Spain by composers and producers familiar with Europop. The boy band performed on popular weekly television shows and released their own movies. Their die-hard fans joked that they had caught "Menuditis." In 1982, Menudo reportedly earned $20 million. For a prefabricated act, that's nothing short of enviable.

However, Menudo was never able to fully cross over to the English-language market, though they made the attempt with three Anglophonic albums. (Maurice Starr was actually recruited to contribute songs to Menudo's attempt at English-language music, but Díaz told him no, that because his Puerto Rican boys couldn't, and this is a direct quote, "feel it the same way that other people, especially black singers, can," Starr's R&B songs wouldn't work for them. He wanted pop songs, an idea Starr took and ran with when he created New Kids on the Block a few years later.)

Menudo broke up in 2009, having featured thirty-nine singers in the boy band's thirty-year career. Their influence on subsequent groups is undeniable and, unfortunately, underserved in the greater boy band conversation. That's an experience no one knows better than the men of New Edition.

IF IT ISN'T LOVE, IT'S NEW EDITION

In 1978, three boys from Orchard Park, in Roxbury, inner-city Boston—the fresh-faced, elementary school–aged Bobby Brown, Michael Bivins, and Ricky Bell—started a vocal group with two additional neighborhood pals who left almost as quickly as they joined, Travis Pettus and Corey Rackley. The peewee boy band wanted to make their own spending money by performing small gigs at schools around town, delighting supportive communities with their high-note Motown covers. Not long after Pettus and Rackley decided the shows weren't for them, Brown, Bivins, and Bell were joined by friend Ralph "Rizz" Tresvant and local chore-ographer Brooke Payne's nephew Ronnie DeVoe. As the legend goes, Payne, who met the boys after watching them perform at a local talent show, christened the group New Edition, as in "the new edition of the Jackson 5." He became their first manager.

On November 15, 1981, after coming in second at the Hollywood Talent Night in Boston's Strand Theatre, the quintet managed to impress its organizer, local producer Maurice Starr. Even though the prize for first place was a recording session with Starr and they were the runner-up, he was clearly enamored with them. (The winners were a rap group, anyway, and Starr wanted to work with a black bubblegum-pop band.) He signed the boys to his Streetwise Records and gave them a song he was working on called "Candy Girl." With Starr behind them, in March 1983, New Edition released their debut LP, also called *Candy Girl*. They became local heroes virtually overnight. By April, the title track had hit number 17 on the Billboard Hot 100 and number 1 on the Billboard hot black singles chart. They became heroes in a lot of other places, too.

New Edition felt like they were on top of the world or, at least, Boston. Ready to embark on their first national stint playing to new audiences across the country, a tour bus pulled up into the projects that summer and brought the boys face-to-face with their new lives as touring musicians. It was grueling work. When the tweens returned home a few months later, feeling like they really were the Jackson 5 (at least, as dog-tired as the Motown act probably felt all the time), Bobby, Michael, Ricky, Ronnie, and Ralph optimistically opened checks for tour and *Candy Girl* album sales that totaled a dismal $1.87, presented to them as effects of "recoupment." In New Edition's 2005 VH1 *Behind the Music* episode, Starr explained, "people think I've got these guys' money. The booking agent sent the money directly to them, and whatever

my percentage was, they sent to me…I did not take their money."
After seeking damages in a legal battle that settled out of court,
the group cut ties with Starr and Streetwise Records.

In 1984, New Edition signed to MCA Records and released
their self-titled second album with hits like the '80s electro-pop
"Cool It Now" and the middle school crush ballad "Mr. Telephone
Man," written by Ray Parker Jr. (yes, the *Ghostbusters* theme song
guy). Unsurprising to anyone who heard it,
but surprising given their circumstance, it
sold really well and was certified double
platinum by 1985. They were stars.
Sonically, the record was straight-up pop,
and New Edition, now full-on teenagers,
felt it wasn't totally their speed. They
craved a bit more edge, a bit more rebelliousness.
Simultaneously, Ralph Tresvant was made the de facto front man
of the group (Bell sang lead prior to "Candy Girl") and the others
grew increasingly unsettled with the unbalanced power dynamic.
I should clarify: everyone was unhappy, but Bobby Brown was
pissed. He hated New Edition's public-facing innocent image.

Then, this: in 1985 New Edition learned the contract they had
signed with MCA Records wasn't actually with the label at all. They
were tethered to a company called Jump & Shoot Productions,
a trap that befalls many first-time music industry hopefuls. The
boy band found themselves in a production deal instead of a
record deal, an exploitative agreement in which a middleman takes
profits from an act and can decide when, where, and how much
to pay musicians for their work, labor, and royalties. To give you
a sense of how bad an arrangement like that actually is, in the
Behind the Music special, New Edition's 1985–1997 tour manager

Jeff Dyson referred to the deal as "legalized slavery." To get out of the contract, the boys had to borrow a considerable amount from MCA. Instead of simply being broke, they took on untenable amounts of debt.

To pay off what they owed, the group was pushed through an accelerated schedule, only intensifying their interpersonal conflict. In the winter of 1985, New Edition released their third full-length LP, *All for Love*. The next month, the boys, tired of Bobby Brown's showboating and attention-seeking, provocative performances, voted him out of the band. (In a 2017 episode of *Oprah: Where Are They Now?*, New Edition revealed that Brown's on-stage antics weren't the only reason for their decision. The band was under industry pressure to get rid of Brown. Ricky Bell said, "The way that it was presented to us at the time was if we didn't get rid of him, everything was in jeopardy.") The following year, Brown released his debut solo album, the not-so-subtle *King of the Stage*. It didn't do well. Brown was still singing what felt like New Edition songs and had not yet found his footing as a solo artist despite his desire to make it on his own. New Edition's first and only album as a quartet, an entire album of doo-wop covers called *Under the Blue Moon*, out the same year, performed only decently by their standards. It went gold.

New Edition's woes only intensified from there. (Are you sensing a pattern here?) This time, it was boy band competition in the form of a bunch of playful Caucasian kids their former producer Maurice Starr put together with the aim that they would become "the white New Edition," called New Kids on the Block. Ralph Tresvant, too, thought about pursuing a solo project like Brown before him, a move that would prove to be common in most ensuing boy band stories: once one goes, fracturing is inevitable.

With Ralph's impending exit, another lead vocalist, Johnny Gill from Washington, D.C., was invited to join the group. And he did, for a while. Except Tresvant hadn't actually left New Edition, and they became a quintet once again. Gill contributed vocals on their 1988 smooth new jack swing LP, *Heart Break*, New Edition's first time working with the production dream team of Jimmy Jam and Terry Lewis, known for their work on Janet Jackson's *Control*. The album went platinum in three months. Soon, New Edition was able to pay off their debts.

Gill stuck with the group until 1990, when New Edition embarked on an indefinite hiatus. In that time, Ricky Bell, Michael Bivins, and Ron DeVoe formed a trio called Bell Biv DeVoe (BBD). The "Poison" group would go on to have a successful R&B career, but nothing like Bobby Brown, whose second LP, *Don't Be Cruel*, released the same day as *Heart Break*, went seven times platinum. Justin Timberlake, eat your heart out.

Eventually New Edition would reunite in 1996, in the midst of the next wave of boy band fever, but not for very long. Every once in a while, the group will crop up in new and exciting ways: brief appearances here, a multipart biographical docuseries on BET there. Though they never fully received the mainstream notability of the Jackson 5 before them or New Kids on the Block afterward, New Edition was the definitive boy band, setting the stage for all who followed.

THE WHITE NEW EDITION: NEW KIDS ON THE BLOCK

After cutting ties with New Edition, the group he helped legiti-
mize, and quitting the music industry for two weeks, Maurice Starr
was determined to win the boy band game by creating another
group that could compete with Bobby Brown and crew. This time,
he wanted to take it a step further and build a band that could
conquer the mainstream. What New Edition was for black youth,
Starr wanted to engineer with white boys that could be marketed
as a pop act for Top 40 America. In 1984, with the help of music
manager Mary Alford, known for her work with funk rock star
Rick James, he eventually found them: rapper Donnie Wahlberg;
Donnie's best friend, break dancer Danny Wood; brothers Jonathan
and Jordan Knight; and the youngest member, the Michael
Jackson—channeling Joey McIntyre. Together, they were known to
the world as New Kids on the Block.

The boys checked every box on Starr's list, including the
most exigent one: they were white boys from Boston's Dorchester
neighborhood who grew up listening to black music, a direct
result of the city's Racial Imbalance Act. Passed in 1965, the law
required any school with a population of more than
50 percent of one race to desegregate through
busing. Coincidentally, most of NKOTB
attended black public schools in Roxbury,
the same community that created New
Edition, where they learned of the bustling
b-boy scene. They were obsessed with
R&B, funk, and the earliest rap records.
Turning these guys into the white New
Edition was kind of like shooting fish in a
barrel. Starr couldn't have gotten luckier.

DONNIE

As the well-documented NKOTB folklore goes, on his thir-
teenth birthday, Donnie Wahlberg entered Strawberries Records
in Boston's Downtown Crossing neighborhood and found himself
struggling to decide between two purchases: would he pick
up New Edition's first record, *Candy Girl*, or something by the
Afrofuturistic electro-funk Jonzun Crew, *Lost in Space*, two acts
from his city? He examined both LPs and noticed each record
had Maurice Starr's name on the back. Whatever the motivation,
Donnie bought the sci-fi Jonzun LP that day. The next summer, he'd
find himself in Starr's home, performing for the producer. After an
informal audition, Starr promised to make him famous.

It was Alford who convinced Starr to first check out the then
fourteen-year-old Donnie for his white boy band project. When
Wahlberg made his way to Starr's Roxbury rowhouse with his
brother Mark and some neighborhood friends that fated day,
Starr was so impressed he actually asked both Wahlbergs to join
a group he called NYNUK (pronounced *nah-nuke*), a nonsensical
term he made up and never fully explained. (My favorite fan theory
is that the name was taken from the title of a 1922 docudrama
about the lives of an Inuit family living in the Arctic circle titled
Nanook of the North. My personal theory is that it is probably a
simple acronym of some sort, like, **N**ew **Y**ear **N**ew Yo**u**, **K**ids!) They
agreed. From there on out, the Wahlberg boys would go to Starr's
home every weekend to rehearse, but Mark quickly lost interest
and dropped out of the project altogether. (He would found the
hip-hop group Marky Mark and the Funky Bunch a few years
later before becoming a celebrated actor.) The hunt for members
commenced: Mark's friend Jamie Kelly joined. Jordan Knight, after
showcasing his break-dancing talent and ineffable falsetto, and his
brother Jonathan, jealous of his sibling's potential celebrity, also

JOEY

signed up. Danny Wood, having shot down Donnie multiple times about NYNUK, finally decided to audition. Once the Knight brothers were on board, he was in, too. After a rowdy debut performance at the Lee School in Dorchester, where the group of "crazy white boys," as they were known, played for a black audience, it became clear that Jamie was not as dedicated to seeing the band through as the others. He quit, and twelve-year-old New Edition superfan Joey McIntyre took the final slot. He was much younger than the other boys and on Father's Day in 1985, he officially joined the band. Naturally, he was greeted with hazing from his teenage colleagues. No wonder his nickname is rumored to have become "Wedgie."

Before becoming New Kids on the Block, NYNUK—shy guy Jon, heartthrob Jordan, the cute one Joey, bad boy Donnie, and big bro Danny—rehearsed incessantly and took on any gig they could, including stints in retirement homes, schools, community centers, roller rinks, and, according to Nikki Van Noy's *New Kids on the Block: Five Brothers and a Million Sisters*, the prison where one of Donnie's brothers was incarcerated. (It's hard to imagine, say, the Jonas Brothers busting it down in Rikers Island, but NYNUK were much more street savvy than your average boy band. They tossed out packs of cigarettes to inmates and won them over. It's all about knowing your audience.) To say they were a low-budget operation for a few years would be an understatement. No capital was coming in, but the group did manage to shock a few crowds, which set them apart and eventually drew industry interest. There were no other white boys break dancing and rapping at the time, after all. In 1986, Columbia (then known as CBS) Records signed the band to its black division, despite the fact that they weren't. Legend has it the VP of the division, Ruben Rodriguez, played it cool and got his shoes shined during their first meeting, while CBS Records senior vice president Larkin Arnold suggested they adopt New Kids on the Block as their new name, taken from the title of one of the group's few original songs. The name fit, and so did the label, and the New Kids released their eponymous debut album in 1986.

It didn't do numbers. (Those would arrive later. By 1990, it would go three-times platinum.) In 1988, after workshopping new edgy choreography, looks, and hands-on involvement in their songs' production to become less about Jackson 5/New Edition worship and more themselves, New Kids released their second LP, *Hangin' Tough*. In April, the first single from the record was released, the perfectly pleasant "Please Don't Go Girl," starring Joey's prepubescent voice. It flopped—that is, until Tampa, Florida's Q105 radio DJ Randy Kabrich accidentally played the single on his modern pop program instead of the hip-hop, R&B, and urban radio stations the song had been circulating in. (In the beginning, New Kids hoped to make it on black radio before crossing over into white radio.) Kabrich's listeners loved the tune, and "Please Don't Go Girl" became the station's most requested song. Realizing their backward marketing scheme was, hello, *backward*, CBS changed focus

JORDAN

and began airing New Kids' videos on networks other than BET. In a matter of months, they were opening for '80s teen icon Tiffany, and their next two singles, "You Got It (The Right Stuff)" and "I'll Be Loving You (Forever)," went straight to Top 40 radio stations. They were undeniable hits with her crowd, which quickly became their own.

By December of that year, *Hangin' Tough* was certified seven-times platinum. And unlike New Edition before them, their contracts were solid. New Kids on the Block were rich.

Their timing was perfect. When the New Kids arrived on the scene, popular music was reserved for machismo-dripping, dick-in-your-face hair metal. It was the bro-centric golden age of Whitesnake, Def Leppard, Skid Row, and Poison. Pop music was owned by Paula Abdul, Madonna, George Michael, and Milli Vanilli. New Kids filled a vacuum in the market and on the radio: cute, jovial boys who could sing and dance, and did so specifically for young women. Soon, their faces were on everything: posters, dolls, shoelaces, bedding, toys, marbles, school supplies, T-shirts, and later, a popular clothing line at thriving mall retailer JCPenney. Merchandising became their legacy.

In June 1990, New Kids dropped their fourth pop album, *Step by Step* (their third was a Christmas album titled *Merry, Merry Christmas*; there's no need to expound upon that further). *Step by Step*'s title track would become the best-selling record of their career, spending three weeks at number 1 on the Billboard Hot 200 despite the fact that the album was recorded haphazardly on the road, while

JONATHAN

the band was touring, and that the boys didn't even really like it very much. Donnie wanted to rap more aggressively, but the New Kids team was worried about losing its white audience. Obviously, this was painfully pre–Eminem and Vanilla Ice, and they didn't have the edge of the Beastie Boys. By the end of the year, New Kids on the Block were the highest-paid entertainers in the country. They had also grown to resent one another.

DANNY

The total lack of privacy that accompanies fame, and the ridicule they experienced from an increasingly boy band–hating press, really got to the group. They started traveling on separate buses. What was once fun had become repetitive, isolating, draining. Not only that, but by the early '90s, American popular culture had moved on from their boy band sound. Grunge would soon intrigue disaffected youth, and a world run by Nirvana doesn't really leave much room for New Kids on the Block. The year 1991 ended on a low note: Donnie was arrested in Louisville, Kentucky, for setting fire to a hotel room, but the charges were eventually dropped. In reality, he simply sprayed the area with a fire extinguisher, but tabloids aren't into nuance when it comes to boy bands behaving badly. In December, New Kids symbolically threw in the towel by releasing a greatest hits album, the all too apropos *H.I.T.S.*

The boys continued to grow apart from one another and eventually from Maurice Starr, whom Jon Knight described to Noy as "becoming more and more delusional and cocky—doing interviews that put us in a bad light." The producer began wearing military dress uniforms meant for official ceremonies as both an eccentricity and a move meant to establish authority. New Kids on the Block parted ways with him in 1992. "After *Step by Step*, it was over. We didn't need him anymore, plain and simple," Jordan said in *New Kids on the Block: Five Brothers and a Millions Sisters*. "He was just saying weird things in the media, acting crazy in the general suit, his stuff was getting cheesier and cheesier. It was just all done." To further distance themselves, the band released their fifth and final pre-reunion album, 1994's *Face the Music*, under the acronymic name NKOTB. The record was an R&B return to roots without the pop sheen; a self-serious, adult album without much commercial viability. Even the cover art, a black-and-white photograph of the tired guys mean mugging near one another, felt forced. Jonathan, unhappy, suffering from generalized anxiety, and navigating his homosexuality, quit the band. After the *Face the Music* tour concluded, the whole of New Kids decided to call it quits, too.

Each member went on to settle into life post–boy band. They started families, they moved around, and most of them continued to pursue artistic goals: Donnie, who married noted anti-vaxxer Jenny McCarthy, had a role in the 1999 cult classic *The Sixth Sense* and began acting full-time, eventually landing the part of Danny Reagan on the popular 2010s cop show *Blue Bloods*. In the late '90s, Danny, Joey, and Jordan all pursued solo music careers. The latter two were decently successful (Jordan's 1999 solo single "Give It to You" hit number 10 on the Billboard Hot 100), but it was rough for them. The Backstreet Boys and *NSYNC had taken over, and there wasn't much room for teen pop nostalgia just yet.

In 2008, NKOTB officially reunited as a quintet. Jonathan was back on board, and they announced their return on the *Today* show. That fall, they released their first album in fourteen years, *The Block*, on Interscope Records and were right back in the swing of things, finally on their own terms. They launched an annual fan cruise full of performances, meet and greets, and more, which other boy bands would ape in later decades. In 2011 and 2012, they toured with Backstreet Boys as NKOTBSB, raking in $40 million in its first year alone. In 2013, they released another album, the pop-rock *10*, as independent artists.

More self-aware than most boy bands by the year 2019, New Kids released the droll single, "Boys in the Band," accomplishing what this book hopes to do: a quick, hook-heavy chronology of modern boy band history, only their version is delivered in a little over four minutes, with Donnie spitting the raps he always dreamed of: "Let's go back to the beginning, pay respect / New Edition / Then came BBD, BSB, B2K, 1D / 98 Degrees / Come and talk to me, Jodeci / From B Brown to Beantown / To H-Town to O-Town / Came the sound Berry Gordy found all the way back in Motown (woo) / Ah, had to catch my breath / Peace / LFO, Menudo, JLS, BTS / Westlife, Jackson 5, *NSYNC, Take That / I want you back!"

If New Kids took what New Edition created and expanded it to such great heights, they not only laid the foundation for forthcoming boy band megastars, they also taught them how to merchandise, reunite, and throw a mean cruise, too. Who doesn't want to sail the high seas with their favorite boy band? That's the stuff of fan fiction.

Style Watch

NEW KIDS' FASHION is best described as "sporty casual" or "streetwear." That changed when stylist Patrick Petty began putting Donnie in J Brand jeans and John Varvatos suits as an adult, but when NKOTB were boys, they dressed like it. The most hilarious example of their adventurous attire is Joey in the "Hangin' Tough" video, which I'm allowed to poke fun at because he is much richer than I could ever hope to be.

* Donnie wore his fair share of backward baseball caps in the group's early days, but no piece of headwear beats the black top hat McIntyre wore in the music video for their biggest smash. Not only does it appear as if he has robbed an Abraham Lincoln museum gift shop, but the top part, the crown, has been completely removed—purposefully ripped off to reveal his locks. I assume this was meant to give him some street cred, but what child owns headgear meant for the opera?

* New Kids always rocked jerseys or T-shirts. Jordan's Batman tee in the "I'll Be Loving You Forever" video is legendary, but I'm partial to the smiley shirt Joey was instructed to wear. It's classic, in a sleepy stoner way. The only '80s design that could top it would be a California Raisins print. He's also wearing a leather jacket because the smile was probably a little too inviting to leave fully exposed, you know? He's supposed to look tough. Tough guys wear moto gear.

* There were two pants options for NKOTB: slightly oversize acid-wash jeans or shorts. Here, Joey's in jeans.

* New Kids were sort of infamous for their sneakers, mostly Nike and Adidas kicks. They might be ideal for the basketball court, but they're a dancer's best friend, too.

TECH TOCH:
Fan Mail to Fan Clubs

LONG BEFORE SOCIAL media gave boy band members the luxury of interacting directly with their fans and the displeasure of communing with their venomous detractors at the touch of a few buttons, options were limited to in-person conversations at meet and greets, snail mail, and actually talking on the phone. If you wanted to reach the object of your musical affection, you wrote to an address provided in the liner notes of the physical record by the major label or a PO box listed in a teen magazine, or, if you were resourceful, allergic to social boundaries, and lived in the same region as your fave boy band, you cracked open the Yellow Pages and searched for a family name. In the beginning of New Kids on the Block, as is boy band tradition, the guys' mothers would answer their letters. (George Harrison's mom, Louise, famously took on that underappreciated duty in the Beatles' early days, and getting a response from her was nearly as exciting as hearing from the guys themselves. Boy band moms are a subject study all their own.) By spring of 1989, Nikki Van Noy writes, the New Kids' moms were so overwhelmed by fan mail, they began sending copied letters. It only grew from there. Young girls, thrilled to have received something, anything from their beloved boy band, began writing more and more frequently on the off chance they'd receive a second, third, or fourth response. Whether or not it was an original seemed to be an afterthought. Eventually New Kids on the Block's manager, Dick Scott, stepped in and begged the moms to stop responding in an effort to curb the fanaticism. They did, but only when they were unable to keep up with the unruly quantity of inquiries. As a result, the New Kids' parents formed the group's official fan club in a rented office building south of Dorchester to help keep things organized.

The New Kids on the Block fan club became a major avenue for fans of the band to feel a certain closeness with the group and to maintain regular updates with what was going on with them. When the band broke up in 1994, Noy notes, the fan club sent its members a letter announcing the club's disbandment and thanked fans for their dedication. When the band began pursuing solo careers, former fan club members joined email lists, message boards, and digital fan forums to keep in contact. Eventually New Kids would relaunch their official fan club—online, for a $69.95 premium membership fee—called Block Nation. When social media took over, the reunited members of New Kids on the Block fully embraced any and all new technology that allowed them the kind of familiarity with their fans never thought of as possible in their golden age, including the dense cesspool that is Twitter.

CHAPTER FOUR

LARGER THAN LIFE: THE BACKSTREET BOYS

IN THE LATE 1980s, in Orlando, Florida—a town built of theme parks and the dreams of stage moms—an extraordinarily wealthy, villainous entrepreneur named Lou "Big Poppa" Pearlman found himself standing on the edge of the music biz. After chartering a few flights for New Kids on the Block on one of his $250,000-a-month planes, which the group paid for in cash, Pearlman grew intrigued by their success, and then greedy. NKOTB was the biggest boy band on the planet, and their team told Pearlman they took home $800 million in merchandise and $200 million in concert sales. Pearlman internalized that information and decided he was going to get a piece of the action. So, in 1992, he placed a classified ad in the local paper, the *Orlando Sentinel*, looking for cute young boys to mold into a multimillion-dollar empire. It read, TEEN MALE VOCALIST. PRODUCER SEEKS MALE SINGERS THAT MOVE WELL, BETWEEN 16–19 YEARS OF AGE. WANTED FOR NEW KIDS–TYPE SINGING/ DANCE GROUP. SEND PHOTO OR BIO OF ANY KIND.

If your bad-guy radar isn't going off yet, it really should be.

The ad got a response from Denise McLean, mom to the guile-less fourteen-year-old Alexander James "AJ" McLean. He became the first member of an incubating group of guys and quickly adopted the role of resident bad boy. (A worthy excuse, if there is one, for the "69" tattoo he acquired over his belly button later in life. He maintains that it is simply his "lucky number.") After a year of failed hires and lackluster casting calls (including a teen named Charles Edwards, who couldn't carry a tune to save his life, and a kid named Sam Licata, who was too distracted by solo dreams), and with the help of AJ's manager, Jeanne "Tanzy" Williams, Pearlman compiled his guy group: Howie Dorough, eighteen, the loveable biracial teen from up the street whom Pearlman had auditioned previously and knew as Tony Donetti, an almost-member of the Puerto Rican boy band Menudo; Ruskin, Florida's Nick Carter, thir-teen, the baby of the bunch who was too dang charming to pass up, even if he was too young, and who turned down a coveted role on Disney's *All-New Mickey Mouse Club* for the chance to change music forever; and Lexington, Kentucky, cousins Brian Littrell, seventeen, and Kevin Richardson, twenty, the latter of whom was working as Goofy and Aladdin at Walt Disney World at the time. And so, on April 20, 1993, Backstreet Boys (BSB for short) were official, named by Pearlman after Orlando's Backstreet flea market because nothing says "let's get those girls' palms sweating" like the image of an open-air mothball fest and reclaimed wood. A month later, the Backstreet Boys, with newly obtained matching haircuts, made their live debut at SeaWorld's Grad Nite to a crowd of three thousand people.

For the first year of their existence, the boys practiced choreography in a blimp hangar owned by Pearlman. The sad scene

AJ

transformed when Pearlman iced Williams out (she later sued him; they settled for an undisclosed sum) and he hired the Wright Stuff—Johnny Wright, New Kids on the Block's road manager, and his wife, Donna, who suggested the Backstreet Boys hop in a Winnebago and go on a national tour of middle and high schools to seduce unsuspecting teens everywhere with their impeccable harmonies, suggestive choreography, and pitiful peach fuzz. First, BSB had to quit their jobs, move into a house together, and undergo boot camp for boy bands, which included constant dance lessons, vocal exercises, six-to-eight-hour daily rehearsals, and tutors on deck. (It's around this time that Howie, once a lead vocalist of the group, was replaced by Brian and shoved into the background.) Their Motown-like industriousness worked, and in 1994, they had a record deal with major label Jive Records,[*] now known as RCA/Sony.

The label sent them to Stockholm, Sweden, to work with pop production masterminds Denniz PoP (real name Dag Volle) and Max Martin (née Karl Martin Sandberg), known for their work with Ace of Base and Robyn—it was a few years before popular culture accepted the idea that producers are artists themselves. The Backstreet Boys' music changed drastically, defined by the blown-out synthesized screech sound that began their first single, "We've Got It Goin' On" in 1995, and in 1997, their first single

---

[*] The Backstreet Boys almost signed to Mercury Records, but rumor has it that John Cougar Mellencamp threatened to drop the label if they worked with boy bands. In a 2013 interview with the *Dallas Observer*, Nick Carter said he was familiar with the gossip, but "no one knew" who they were at the time. I'm going to choose to believe it. Historically, rock stars and boy bands haven't made good bedfellows.

NICK

to hit in America, "Everybody (Backstreet's Back)." The guys in the band call it an *"erht erht"* noise in the 2015 feature film *Backstreet Boys: Show 'Em What You're Made Of*; I think it most resembles the final buzzer in a high school basketball game partnered with some funky drum and bass. Different strokes.

It took until their second album for Backstreet to insert themselves into the hearts and minds of American teens. Their self-titled debut record was never released in the US, and that's because their timing sucked: New Kids on the Block broke up. The '80s boy band craze had died down. Radio was dominated by serious R&B chanteuses, grunge, Hootie and the Blowfish, Boyz II Men, and old-school hip-hop like Dr. Dre. Sensitive teenage boys with billowy cheeks and simultaneously strong jawlines (how *do* they do that?) weren't making the cut. Luckily enough, Europe was on board and totally lost it when the quintet rolled up in matching red, white, and blue Uncle Sam jerseys. Once they charted in Germany, Switzerland, France, and Austria, it was only a matter of time before the US got the message.

Their second album, 1997's *Backstreet's Back*, and its first single, "Quit Playin' Games (With My Heart)," remedied their America problem. In the video, Brian, Nick, Kevin, Howie, and AJ are total moist beefcakes (sorry), prancing around in fully unbuttoned button-downs, absolutely dosed in rainwater; it is entirely vestal, illustrative of their ability to really emote, *teen girl fodder*, and the horniest thing any young person at the time had ever seen, at least on a boy. Women have been wet since the dawn of time, or the origins of *Sports Illustrated*. Here, the Backstreet Boys were danger-immune sex gods who wore collared shirts, and they were dripping. Needless to say, "Games" climbed to number 2 on the Billboard Hot 100 and kick-started their inevitable US takeover.

By 1998, the Backstreet Boys were an international success story without any wealth. They were making a measly $300,000 each over the course of a four-year career, while Pearlman made $10 million. (I haven't had to do basic math since high school, but I'm pretty sure that comes out to a $75,000 annual salary for a 100+ hour work week, which could explain why they referred to themselves as "indentured servants." Boy bands should unionize.) According to *In Touch* magazine, they were estimated to be worth $50 million apiece. Unknown to the guys, Pearlman financed Backstreet under one of the largest Ponzi schemes of all time, his company Trans Continental Records (Trans Con for short—the writing was on the wall). Not only did he own the boy band, but he controlled most of their assets by listing himself as a sixth member of the group in the fine print of their contract, earning a sixth (and then some) of everything the boy band made. The only way for the Backstreet Boys to get what they were owed, what they were actually earning, was to buy him out. So, they did, to the tune of $29.5 million. In the same year, Brian Littrell, then twenty-three, had open-heart surgery to address a congenital birth defect, his second time undergoing such a procedure (the first was when he was five to correct a heart murmur). Times were challenging.

With Pearlman out of the way, Backstreet was able to produce 1999's *Millennium*, their first number 1 full-length and one of the best-selling albums, ever. The release, which brought into the world such dry hump–ready classics as "I Want It That Way," "Larger Than Life," and

BRIAN

KEVIN

"Show Me the Meaning of Being Lonely," sold over 13 million copies worldwide by February 2001. (That success, mind you, wasn't all organic: Britney Spears's debut album,…*Baby One More Time*, released a few months prior, concluded with a hidden track teaser for *Millennium*. Her fans became their fans, this fan included. It also didn't hurt that the label gave away live *Millennium* CD teasers to grow hype for the band at Burger King. More teen pop acts would do well to go straight to the source—fast-food joints—for promotional purposes.) The Backstreet Boys were not only the biggest boy band on the planet; they became the biggest boy band of all time.

Except there was a problem on the horizon, and they called themselves *NSYNC. Not so secretly, they were another group formed by Pearlman. In 2000, Backstreet released their fourth studio album without a moment's rest, *Black & Blue*, which sold over 1.6 million copies in the United States within its first week. However, those seriously impressive sales were demolished by their rival boy band, *NSYNC, whose second LP, *No Strings Attached*, sold 2.4 million units in its first week, setting a nearly unbreakable record.

Things did eventually slow for Backstreet, though their longevity is nothing short of admirable. After four full-length albums together, a short hiatus in 2002, and an adult contemporary comeback album, *Never Gone*, in 2005, an exhausted Kevin left the group in 2006. He rejoined in 2012, and the band is still active today. Backstreet Boys became one of the few boy bands to beat the five-year curse and build something sustainable, even after all the Pearlman drama. And why not? None of their solo careers really stuck the way they have for other boy band balladeers past and present, and Backstreet's always gonna come back, alright?

NICK CARTER GIRLS
VS.
BRIAN LITTRELL LADIES

IN THE BACKSTREET milieu, fans who used the floppy-haired men to spark their internal flame of teen desire fit into two camps: Nick Carter girls or Brian Littrell ladies. Sure, each member enjoyed crushes of varying degrees (my apologies to the Howie girls reading this; I appreciate and am bewildered by your aspirational dedication to apparent mediocrity), but the Backstreet fan ethos really begins and ends with these two. Carter, the obvious heartthrob, speaks to the ambitious fangirl. She knows she wants the best and she'll settle for nothing less. To her, Carter is the embodiment of the perfect specimen. He's tall, blue-eyed, sweet, Southern, ultimately sexless, a soft boy with a hard six-pack. He's the rose-shaped buttercream icing sprinkled with gold flakes that adorns the most romantic wedding cake in her fantasy marriage to him. You can likely find an image of the sweet dessert doodled in the back of her history textbook. Littrell, on the other hand, is more like the flour foundation. He's practical in a way that would come in handy in any partnership, the kind of no-nonsense fellow teen girls have yet to desire, but women know is husband material.

Carter could never mount a TV, but Littrell would do so without you having to ask him to do the chore. These are things you don't need to be worried about between algebra II and study hall, but it is applicable to the "Communism" chapter skimmed in social studies: Littrell is the Friedrich Engels to Carter's Karl Marx; they wrote the book together, but Carter gets the glory while Littrell holds down the fort and avoids the hardy party. And if that sounds depressing to you, well, you're probably a Nick Carter girl. They're inseparable, anyway, and Littrell doesn't mind the heavy lifting.

Style Watch

EVERY BOY BAND aims for uniformity in their looks with a little individual-istic personality thrown in for flair, but the Backstreet Boys were committed to dressing exactly the same. (Blame it on their Motown influence, or their desire to mimic Boyz II Men. There's a reason "I'll Never Break Your Heart" sounds so similar to "End of the Road," and style is hard.) In the early 2000s, the group began moving away from being robotic imitations of one another, but some consistencies lingered. They are as follows, and as illus-trated by bad boy AJ McLean.

* Most of the Backstreet buds avoided headgear, but AJ went all in, swapping beanies for proto-steampunk goggles, or do-rags, or top hats, or perhaps most canonical of all: a Kangol hat. His hip-hop side was all but jumping out.

* Denim was a staple for these boys, your classic, all-American Levi's, but never formfitting, à la James Dean. They were more like JD, James's grandson,* who dared to look street-smart without ever entering the streets.

* Leather pants are much more of a boy band staple than you'd be wont to think, and in the '90s, the rule was simple: if the trousers are big and baggy, it's stylish. I imagine it must've created a nice breeze on their undercarriage. Those pants didn't do much to make the boys look more aggressive than, say, a litter of golden retriever puppies, and even those dogs don't have a bite as strong as their bark.

* BSB shoes varied from photo shoot to photo shoot, but stayed within the family of basketball sneakers and colored Timberlands, which you might think of as the JNCO jean of shoes. I absolutely do.

---

* This is not a real person, but wouldn't it be so great if it were?

KANGOL HAT, FOR EASILY PURCHASED SWAGGER
OVERSIZED DENIM, ALSO FOR EASILY PURCHASED SWAGGER
AJ MCLEAN
OVERSIZED LEATHER PANTS, SOMEHOW FREE OF IRONY
TIMBERLANDS, SEE KANGOL HAT ABOVE

Conspiracy Corner:
Lou Pearlman

DESCRIBING THE FRAUDULENT behaviors of Lou Pearlman as a "conspiracy" isn't totally accurate, but similar to any smooth talker behind a Ponzi scheme, his truth is obscured like tweenage secrets shared through a made-up language. The pieces are there, but it's impossible to catechize what truly happened if the only ones who understand modified pig Latin lose the key and refuse to cooperate. Simply put, Pearlman was a bullshit artist, a huckster who made millions in insurance fraud and, later, millions more when he robbed his boy bands.

Born in 1954 in Mitchell Gardens, Flushing, Queens, New York, Pearlman was a shy, reclusive kid completely enamored with Goodyear blimps; a cousin of Art Garfunkel; and a relentless liar (as Tyler Gray points out in *The Hit Charade: Lou Pearlman, Boy Bands, and the Biggest Ponzi Scheme in U.S. History*, the Art Garfunkel thing was famously one of the few truths he ever told). In 1980, at twenty-six years old, Pearlman launched a blimp business called Airship Enterprises Ltd., where he managed to acquire and lease a dilapidated, borderline immobile, sixteen-year-old blimp to the then-hoppin' Jordache jeans company. When it crashed, Pearlman collected the insurance money, all $2.5 million of it, beginning what would become a decades-long career of fraud. By 1985, Pearlman launched a new company, the publicly traded Airship International, where he was able to raise $3 million in a public offering, purchase another ancient blimp, and convince McDonald's, MetLife, and other huge brands to advertise with him. He made bank off of little more than his word. In 1989, Pearlman left New York and bought a 6,000-square-foot home in Orlando as well as the Kissimmee, Florida, hangar the Backstreet Boys would practice in.

Then he launched the private Trans Continental Airlines, yet another company, despite not owning the aircraft he promised investors. He used photographs of model airplanes taken at LaGuardia Airport, his hand scrupulously cropped out of the image, as "proof." In those analog days, the pictures were uncanny. Pearlman grew his organization large enough to begin selling stock options and retirement accounts in the airline, all of which were bogus. As would later be revealed, anyone who invested in him lost everything, and most of those who did were seniors who'd relocated to Florida for well-earned retirements they never got to enjoy. He took in over $300 million for those sales. I wasn't kidding when I said the man was villainous.

Whenever Pearlman had a business endeavor that began to look like the sham that it was, he formed a new entity to fund past debts and keep the wheels turning. He lied constantly. Even when he formed *NSYNC in 1995, Pearlman didn't want the Backstreet Boys (or anyone at his Trans Con label) to know, so all accounting documentation listed the new group as "B-5" on the off chance they'd see it. He ultimately screwed over both boy bands—the Backstreet Boys paid their way out of their contract with Pearlman and *NSYNC settled out of court—but he continued to try to launch other projects like LFO, Take 5, the Latino boy band C-Note, a girl group called Innosense, and Nick Carter's younger brother, Aaron Carter, in order to keep fertile music money coming in. When it appeared like boy bands were on the outs, post–Backstreet and *NSYNC, Pearlman still wanted more. So, he created the MTV reality television show Making the Band to give boy band fans exactly what they'd always craved: more access and an inside look into the boy band creation process. Younger performers were willing and ready to sign with him even while his scammer behavior was becoming increasingly more public because, well, it's a music business deal. Those don't come around every day. O-Town came out of the first season of *Making the Band*, but Pearlman was booted off after its debut and replaced by the host you actually remember, Diddy. Instead of boy bands, R&B-pop groups became the focal point.

But once a scammer, always a scammer. Pearlman even bought a modeling agency called Options while it was under investigation by the FBI for swindling money out of thousands of hopefuls just to keep a steady cash flow coming in. Eventually Pearlman's schemes got the better of him, and around Valentine's Day 2007, the FBI issued a warrant for his properties. Upon their arrival on February 15, he was nowhere in sight. His bank fraud totaled somewhere over $200 million, as did his insurance fraud. He was found in Bali later that year and arrested on the spot. Once back in Orlando, Pearlman was sentenced to twenty-five years in prison, where he died in 2016. He was sixty-two years old.

Throughout all his bad business decisions, too, was an undercurrent, a rumor mill, that Pearlman had sexual interest in the young men he promised to make famous. O-Town's Ashley Parker Angel has spoken publicly about one instance in which Pearlman called him up to his room alone and gave him a deep muscle massage that was interrupted by a phone call, allowing him to escape. In the 2019 documentary *The Boy Band Con: The Lou Pearlman Story*, Nikki DeLoach of Innosense described being secretly filmed disrobing and climbing into a tanning bed inside Pearlman's home, footage that was later shown to his boy bands.

She also refused to sign the "sixth man" agreement to be released from the group and Pearlman's control because hidden within the contract was a nondisclosure agreement. A landmark article published by *Vanity Fair* in 2007 titled "Mad About the Boys" alludes to something inappropriate happening between Pearlman and Nick Carter in 1997, which caused Nick to stop staying over at Pearlman's house and his mother, Jane Carter, to call Pearlman a "sexual predator." In that piece, Pearlman's inappropriate behaviors are reported to range from allegations of showing pornographic movies to teenage boys and jumping "naked into their beds in the morning to wrestle and play" to scenes of "young singers seen emerging from his bedroom late at night, buttoning their pants, sheepish looks on their faces."

In 2009, the late Rich Cronin of LFO went on *The Howard Stern Show* and told the host that Pearlman offered him a great opportunity with some major label in Germany, but it came with a catch. "[Pearlman] goes, 'All he wants to do is touch your penis… Pretty much, just touch your penis and you know, play with it,'" he told Stern. "'In college, I was a psychology minor. I'm gonna help you get through it mentally.' He goes, 'Well, think about it, guys. Don't say this to—don't you fucking tell anyone.'"

Every few years a new generation becomes curious about Pearlman and his methodical musical empire, and with new attention comes new information to dig into. But without any confirmation or further investigation, and with his passing, it's unlikely that the public will ever get all the answers. Pearlman is protected by his lies and a healthy dose of disregard for his fellow person. As Gray notes, in his final letter to his only confidant, Tammie Hilton, he wrote, "I'm so pissed that I've been forced into this position of becoming a martyr." Pearlman was delusional, even in death.

POP-PUNK BOY BANDS: BLINK-182, ALL THE SMALL THINGS, AND THE ART OF PARODY

The music video for the Backstreet Boys' single "I Want It That Way" opens with the sound of a jet plane taking off, ascending far above the heads of Brian, Nick, AJ, Kevin, and Howie. They slow-motion stroll into an airport, glide up an airstair on the runway (no easy feat in baggy bondage pants), and board a private plane adorned with their logo. The vocals kick in, and the video cuts to the leather-clad boys moping around the tarmac, crooning about fire, desire, heartache, and mistakes. The image reeks of Pearlman opportunism and his aviation pseudo-business: the camera zooms into escalator steps, fans surround them in a hangar, and the boys hit the skies at the song's end, off to the next destination to be adored. Besides being equally as confounding as the grammatical nightmare that is the song's chorus—"Tell me why / I never wanna hear you say / I want it that way / 'Cause I want it that way"—the music video doesn't actually mean anything, but it does give viewers a visual representation of how moody, sensitive, sensual, and distinctly Jordan Catalano–like the guys were in 1999.

Southern California pop-punk band Blink-182 saw the humor in "I Want It That Way" and parodied it in their own video for their best-known song to date, "All the Small Things." (It also included a satirical mashup of images inspired by *NSYNC, Britney Spears, and Christina Aguilera, but no one forgets the airport.) The same humming roar of the jet engine opens the visual, and the guys rock humorous (albeit borderline homophobic and kink-shaming) interpretations of Backstreet's outfits in diapers and headbands, complete with suggestive thrusting and licking.

Blink's parody of the pop stars was clever on a few levels. The comedy separated them from the virtuous teen pop that

dominated the charts while positioning themselves alongside
Backstreet and their ilk as a delightfully delinquent alternative. (In
turn, they opened the floodgate for the pop-punk and emo implo-
sion that followed in the early 2000s.) It worked: Blink-182 took
home the award for Best Group Video at the 2000 MTV Video
Music Awards, solidifying their place as the world's first pop-punk
boy band. They were as meticulous as Pearlman's projects in their
marketing, too; it's not coincidental that the most pro-women
song in Blink-182's catalog, "All the Small Things," a cheerful ditty
meant to commend the working woman and her hellish life under
laissez-faire capitalism, is the one that made them superstars.
Work sucks, *girl*, they knew.

If the Backstreet Boys were too dental-retainer rock for you, Blink-182 was cut from a similar cloth, with the addition of toilet humor and a mall punk ethos that gets you kicked out of class for making a masturbation joke and Saturday detention for blow job gags despite having never gotten past second base. Blink was a boy band built exclusively of the bad boy archetype. Their rebelliousness, while dripping with the sort of hetero-machismo that attracts bros, was beguiling enough to draw in a young female fan base. Pop-punk groups like Blink-182, those bands who only know how to play palm-muted power chords and sing exclusively through a nasal whine about girls, ultimately replaced boy bands in the mid-'00s, proving that Blink and the bands that followed were always pop stars, after all. They owed a lot to Backstreet, and the Jonas Brothers owed a lot to them. More on that later.

THE BOY BAND EXPLOSION: 98 DEGREES, O-TOWN, B2K, AND THE GROUPS OF YESTERYEAR

The impulse to begin and end any conversation of '90s boy bands with the Backstreet Boys (and *NSYNC—hold your horses, that's the next chapter) is as enticing as nuking the old Hot Pocket in the back of your freezer instead of actually making dinner. The gooey pizza substitute is definitely an easy option after a long workday, but the carb-y canapé beloved by potheads always comes out of the microwave inexplicably flaccid and ultimately less fulfilling than a nutritious home-cooked meal. And, anyway, isn't there a whole world of food out there worth exploring? That is not to say Backstreet Boys are the Hot Pockets of boy bands. At least give them the title of Totino's Pizza Rolls, the pinnacle of frozen after-school treats. They're simply the entry point in the conversation.

The Backstreet Boys' musical explosion was so immediately intoxicating and so obviously profitable that copycat acts soon followed. BSB broke the boy band seal, and artists everywhere wanted a piece of the action. How else do you think Virgin Megastore (RIP, 1971–2009, in America) and Sam Goody (RIP, 1950s–2012) stayed in business for as long as they did?

Unfortunately, those new groups, too, were derided by music journalists and simultaneously exalted by young women and MTV. Needless to say, criticism did not stop budding boy bands from trying their hand at the spotlight. Some of them were even good! Most of them were not. Those are called one-hit wonders. Here are a few of them.

HANSON (1992-?)

Oklahoma brothers Zac, Taylor, and Isaac Hanson formed their family band in 1992, which actually means they pre-date the Backstreet Boys. You know them for bringing into the world the baby-talk chorus "Mmmbop, ba duba dop / Ba du bop, ba duba dop / Ba du bop, ba duba dop / Ba du, yeah-e-yeah," and for aging into handsome adult men better than most boy band rock stars. They never broke up, so if you're so inclined to see handsome adult men goo-goo ga-ga all over some summer festival stage in Calgary, you absolutely can do that.

WERE THEY A ONE-HIT WONDER? Obviously. Name a Hanson tune that is not "MMMBop."

AVENTURA (1994–2010, 2016, 2019–?)

I am fully aware that some people do not believe Bronx-based bachata greats Aventura are a boy band, and I am also fully aware that those people don't know what they're talking about. These Kings of Bachata, as they are known colloquially, fused the popular boy band formula of the time with the sounds of their neighborhood: Dominican music, R&B, and hip-hop. By not restraining themselves to contemporary music stylings, they became timeless, which is why they were able to stay together for nearly two decades when most groups fall victim to the five-year rule.

> **WERE THEY A ONE-HIT WONDER?** Absolutely not, and that's not even including all of Romeo Santos's solo work. All it takes is a quick listen to "Inmortal," "Ella Y Yo," and "Obsesión" to confirm they were far from a flash in the pan.

98 DEGREES (1995–2002, 2012–?)

In 1995, in Los Angeles, Jessica Simpson's future husband Nick Lachey, his brother Drew Lachey, and two guys they knew back in Ohio named Justin Jeffre and Jeff Timmons formed 98 Degrees. The story of the group's big break has changed throughout the years like a game of telephone, but Nick told MuchMusic in 1997 it all goes back to a failed attempt to sneak backstage at a Montell Jordan and Boyz II Men concert. They were hoping to sing a cappella for Boyz II Men when they ran into their manager, who was working with Jordan at the time. 98 Degrees were invited to open for the "This Is How We Do It" singer for a few shows, which later led to Jordan helping them with their demo. Not long after, one of his dancers passed the cut to Motown Records and got 98 Degrees their deal. She doesn't get enough credit.

WERE THEY A ONE-HIT WONDER? Nope. They went multiplatinum, which is kind of the opposite of what happens to one-hit wonders. Off the top of the ol' noggin, a list of thumpers: "I Do (Cherish You)," "Because of You," "The Hardest Thing," and so on. While 98 Degrees were the most traditionally hetero-masculine of the boy bands of the time, their tracks, thematically, can be defined as "following the heart of a shallow boy dedicated to straining a relatively perfect relationship with unnecessary drama." You know, as sensitive boys with broad shoulders do.

LFO (1995–2002, 2009, 2017)

The year is 1995 and a trio of boys who love Abercrombie & Fitch—Rich Cronin, Brad Fischetti, and Devin Lima—join forces to become LFO, Pearlman's latest Trans Continental undertaking. LFO wasn't the first boy band to name themselves with an acronym, but the brevity and unforgettable nature of its three letters has become an international standard for success. Now that boy bands and pop music are global, three letters promote universal comprehension. Those who don't speak English can readily discuss the group. Plus, back in the day, LFO was quick to type on AOL instant messenger, saving room for important information, like emoticons. Plus, it helps to forget that LFO stands for "Lyte Funkie Ones."

WERE THEY A ONE-HIT WONDER? As much as I imagine everyone reading this to disagree…no? The quirky, lyrically nonsensical "Summer Girls" (ex: "The great Larry Bird, jersey thirty-three /

When you take a sip / You buzz like a hornet / Billy Shakespeare wrote / A whole bunch of sonnets") is by far their most famous tune, but "Every Other Time" and "Girl on TV" were radio hits, too. Jennifer Love Hewitt was the inspiration for "Girl on TV," and she also starred in the music video. If they weren't total luminaries, do you think the Ghost Whisperer would've showed up? If you were to judge popularity based on my favorite measurement—"How many of their songs are available at karaoke?"—the answer is "Almost always all three." They're a three-hit wonder.

C-NOTE (1997–2008, BUT NOT ACTIVE FOR MOST OF THE '00s)

Just as R&B man bands were taking off in the 1990s, so were Latinx crossover acts like Marc Antony, Ricky Martin, Enrique Iglesias, Jennifer Lopez, and for the first half of the decade before her tragic assassination, *mi reina* and yours, Selena Quintanilla-Pérez. After catching the quartet C-Note (which stands for Create Nothing Other Than Excellence; subtlety wasn't in their nature) at a local talent show, Lou Pearlman decided he wanted to add a Latino band to his repertoire and signed the group: Andrew "Dru" Rogers, Jose "Brody" Martinez, Raul Molina from the Dominican Republic, and the half-Cuban, half–Puerto Rican hunk David Perez.

WERE THEY A ONE-HIT WONDER? If that? If it weren't rude as hell, I'd designate them a "no-hit wonder," but they did have one song break into the Billboard Mainstream Top 40. Their first single, 1999's sensual "Wait Till I Get Home," peaked at number 33. For other boy bands, that wouldn't be a success by any stretch of the imagination, but it's more than most could ever hope to achieve, and honestly, I'm not one to talk. The song is good.

B2K (1998–2004, 2018–?)

In the 1990s, black R&B man bands, such as Bell Biv DeVoe, Boyz II Men, 112, Jagged Edge, and Mint Condition, and multiracial groups, such as Color Me Badd and, later, Nu Flavor, enjoyed a series of successful Top 40 crossovers (for example: Blackstreet's platinum-selling "No Diggity," featuring Dr. Dre, hit number 1 on the Billboard Hot 100 and stayed there for a month). Why, then, wasn't there an influx of black R&B boy bands atop the charts (Another Bad Creation, Soul for Real, and bad boys Jodeci excluded), especially when the majority of the white groups at the top were pulling from black music? Producer Chris Stokes,* known for his work with Brandy, decided to get in on the action and came up with a plan: get a bunch of young kids with swagger, build a boy band, and fill the void. In the early 1990s, he managed Immature. In the late '90s, it was all about B2K. The name was a play on "Y2K," or "Boys of the New Millennium," as they referred to themselves. B2K was Omarion, J-Boog, Raz-B, and Lil' Fizz, which formed in 1998, disbanded in 2004, and reunited in 2018. Stokes's system worked: B2K's self-titled debut album peaked at number 1 on the charts. They had a few Top 10 hits, they starred in the 2004 dance classic film *You Got Served*, and its members went on to have solo careers. Also, Omarion and Fizz became stars of VH1's smash show *Love and Hip-Hop: Hollywood*, a program I have wasted entire days binge watching.

WERE THEY A ONE-HIT WONDER? Sort of? There is no doubt that "Bump Bump Bump" was a hit and a half—not to mention, placed on the preferred playlist of every middle school dance in the early to mid-'00s, the first "grinding" track for an

---

* It would be a great oversight not to include the years-long abuse allegations that have clouded B2K and Chris Stokes. In 2007, Raz-B accused Stokes of sexual molestation while he was underage, claims Stokes vehemently denied in an interview with MTV. "I'm not gay. And I'm married. And I have four kids. I been (sic) with my wife for sixteen years. And I'm not a child molester," he said. "So those are all false allegations." Omarion issued a statement around the same time claiming that Raz-B was "lying regarding Chris Stokes...I have spent countless hours, days, weeks and months with the man, since the age of 5, and have never once seen him behave inappropriately." The next day, Raz-B retracted his abuse allegations. Then, in 2008, R&B singer and Raz-B

innumerable amount of seventh graders—and "Uh Huh" is an earworm, too, but their other singles didn't have the same kind of staying power.

DREAM STREET (1999–2002)

In 1999, New York bubblegum band of literal children Dream Street formed with some questionable objectives in mind: hold a girl's hand, hear a silly love song in her heart, and take her for a walk down the Milky Way. Scientific inconsistencies aside, the quintet broke up less than four years after forming because of a dispute between the group's parents and their managers. (Long story short: the parents alleged Dream Street's team urged them "to have sexual relations with teen-age girls" and exposed them to booze and pornography.) The disbandment turned out to be a blessing for front man Jesse McCartney, who'd go on to have a respectable career as a solo artist and songwriter. He's partially responsible for Leona Lewis's 2007 bop "Bleeding Love," which you've absolutely heard at a wedding recently. Righteous.

labelmate Quindon Tarver told *Vibe Magazine*, "For a certain amount of years, I was molested. I wouldn't say exactly by Chris [Stokes], but he would organize it. He'd organize activities to be done as he sat and watched…He would make another member of [the boy band Immature] like come and do things…Oh my God. Four years. It was rough." In 2010, Raz-B posted a video of him and Tarver discussing similar alleged abuses, such as purportedly being coerced into showering with other boys. Tarver released a statement saying he "had no clue our conversation was being recorded, nor did I know it would wound [sic] up on the internet. I was under the impression that Raz-B and myself were having a private conversation, nothing more or less."

WERE THEY A ONE-HIT WONDER? Hard to tell. "It Happens Every Time" got a lot of play on Radio Disney, but they also had a handful of songs in popular movies, like *Pokémon: The Movie 2000* (which also featured O-Town and Christian boy band Plus One). I'm going to say yes, but a soft yes, the kind you let out when your friend asks you a question after a long-winded story you checked out of fifteen minutes ago.

THE MEATY CHEESY BOYS (1999–2001)

The apogee of boy bands brought about endless parody (and probably could've ended with MTV's satirical 2Gether, their 2000 single "U + Me = Us (Calculus)" and the rapped lyric "Girl, algebra, trigonometry / Can never equal up to what you do to me / So let's integrate / Don't differentiate"), but who could've guessed fast-food chain Jack in the Box would create their own mega-successful group for televised ads? Or that it would work? The Meaty Cheesy Boys—TK, JT, TJ, EJ, and another EJ—took the manu-factured bit and used it to sell hamburgers to teenagers and, man, did they have hooks. Despite the fact that none of them were actual singers and the whole thing was a sham, the Meaty Cheesy Boys' model-like members were approached for real-life record deals, which speaks volumes about the state of the industry. Don't confuse them with the Spicy Crispy Sandwich Girls, who were the girl group equivalent and also very real. Oh, and fun fact: one of the EJs was portrayed by Wade Robson, Britney Spears's longtime choreographer.

WERE THEY A ONE-HIT WONDER? Not sure. Those commercials are unfailing. If you watched a lot of American television in 1999–2001, you might recall their hits "Let's Go Get Some Fries" and "You Are the One." Also, they performed "Ultimate Cheeseburger" at the 1999 Billboard Music Awards, so you be the judge.

O-TOWN (2000–2003, 2014–?)

Blink in 2000, and you might've missed O-Town. The quintet, made up of Ashley Parker Angel, Erik-Michael Estrada, Trevor Penick, Jacob Underwood, and Ikaika Kahoano (who was almost immediately replaced by Dan Miller), formed in Orlando and named themselves after the city despite the fact that no member of the group hailed from there. (The power of Pearlman, eh?) They were guinea pigs of sorts, managed by Big Poppa Lou and assembled for the debut season of *Making the Band*. They toured with Britney Spears but never really established themselves as memorable. They broke up in 2003 and reunited a decade later, but nothing has really stuck.

WERE THEY A ONE-HIT WONDER? Let's go with two-hit wonder. "Liquid Dreams" is a close second to "All or Nothing," but for the most part, that's it.

THE ENGLISH BOY BAND EXPLOSION: TAKE THAT, BOYZONE, AND MORE, YA ANGLOPHILE

Boy bands tend to get their foothold across the pond before blowing up in the United States, and I haven't even touched upon One Direction yet. In the 1990s, Europe was all about these gentle boys of varying cavorting ability, and no place was vying for their own movement of accented hunks more than the UK. The decade sparked a golden age for English boy bands like it did in the US, and before you ask: historians have yet to weigh in on why all the group names sound like exclusive discotheques or restaurant-clubs Carrie and the girls frequented on *Sex and the City*. Come on, *Blue*? Really? (Or, in the case of "Caught in the Middle" one-hit wonders A1, steak sauce.) Perhaps there's a sexiness English boy bands could get away with that their prudish American counterparts could not. I mean, if you played any of these groups at your first boy-girl party in middle school, things were bound to get interesting. Spin the bottle, anyone? Someone's gotta snog.

TAKE THAT (1989–1996, 2005–?)

Mancunian boy band Take That, the project of prodigal song-writer Gary Barlow, Howard Donald, Mark Owen, Jason Orange, and Robbie Williams, got together in 1989 when manager Nigel Martin-Smith decided he wanted to create an English boy band à la New Kids on the Block. While they were massive overseas—it's not so much that they were the English Backstreet Boys, but that the Backstreet Boys were the American Take That—the group never made it in the States. By the time Clive Davis signed them to his Arista Records label in 1995, Williams, already a fledging soloist, quit the band. Take That were on the outs and a few years

too early to enjoy the boy band movement in the US (at the time, Americans were mourning Kurt Cobain, and treacly pop just didn't have a place yet), but their legacy stays unimpeachable across the Atlantic.

WERE THEY A ONE-HIT WONDER? I can say with full confidence they absolutely were not a one-hit wonder, and anyone who argues otherwise has not spent much time communicating with Brits, Western Europeans, and/or Australians enough to prove it. Take a seat for this one: Take That's debut album stayed in the UK Top 75 chart for seventy-three weeks. That's nearly a year and a half. They were colossal. Even Americans have cried to "Back for Good" and its dripping wet black-and-white music video that's totally proto-Backstreet's "Quit Playin' Games (With My Heart)." At least, they've heard it a few dozen times on adult contemporary radio.

EAST 17 (1991–1999, 2006–?)

East 17, the foursome of Tony Mortimer, Brian Harvey, Terry Coldwell, and John Hendy, was one of the most popular English boy bands in the 1990s. Astonishingly, they stayed together for nearly a decade. The group meshed Europop, '90s rave culture, and hip-hop in an unexpected way, which makes it pretty difficult to believe they were positioned against Take That in some English version of the Backstreet vs. *NSYNC rivalry. "House of Love," unlike anything Gary Barlow wrote, is a club-ready hit meant for teens and, unsurprisingly, it performed really well in Scandinavia. For some, East 17 was a gateway into the life sentence that is getting really, seriously into techno, something no one can say any other boy band has accomplished. (Also, their Christmas song "Stay Another Day" is kind of great.)

WERE THEY A ONE-HIT WONDER? No way. When a group stays together as long as East 17, including their reunion in 2006, lightning strikes more than once. And thunder sounds like "Uhn Tiss Uhn Tiss Uhn Tiss."

BOYZONE (1993–2000, 2007–2019)

Boyzone, the Irish boy band created by Louis Walsh (who later became Westlife's manager and an *X Factor* judge), got their start in 1993. Keith Duffy, Stephen Gately, Mikey Graham, Ronan Keating, and Shane Lynch came together after answering an ad put out by Walsh in their native Dublin; he wanted to put together an Irish version of the recently disbanded Take That. Boyzone was, well, exactly *that*, a diluted, reincarnated Take That with slight alterations. What the group lacked in flash, however, they made up for in brooding. They're basically a band built exclusively of *Gilmore Girls'* Jess Mariano types.

> **WERE THEY A ONE-HIT WONDER?** Absolutely not. Have you heard "Picture of You"? Or "No Matter What"? The throwback "Love Me for a Reason"? "I'll Never Not Need You," written by the great Diane Warren? Come on.

5IVE (FIVE) (1997–2001, 2006–2007, 2013–?)

Who doesn't love a boy band name that requires no deciphering? On the nose, the lot of 'em. 5ive, the London-based group, had five members: Ritchie Neville, Scott Robinson, Richard Abidin "Abs, Abz, Abz Love" Breen, J. Brown, and Sean Conlon. The boy band hit the scene right after Take That disbanded and quickly occupied the space Robbie Williams and crew left vacant. Christened "the Spice Boys" (they shared a team with the Spice Girls, Safe Management's Chris and Bob Herbert, the latter of whom signed the group after they responded to a casting call), 5ive worked with Max Martin and Denniz PoP. In that regard, they were like Backstreet Boys and *NSYNC, but they altered the Swede-pop sound by throwing in hip-hop elements, foreshadowing future boy bands' hybrid approach to genre.

WERE THEY A ONE-HIT WONDER? Nope. Fans of 5ive love a handful of their tracks and not just the ones that charted, either, like "When the Lights Go Out" and "Slam Dunk (Da Funk)."

BBMAK (1997–2003, 2018–?)

On paper, Liverpudlian trio BBMak (a nonsense term taken from the first letter of the boys' last names: Christian **B**urns, Mark **B**arry and Stephen **Mc**Nally) doesn't seem very boy band–esque. There are only three of them, they all play instruments, and instead of touring high schools across their country in their earliest days like New Edition, they were on the British pub and bar circuit until signing to Disney's Hollywood Records and inevitably dropping their biggest hit, "Back Here." All of their massive, melodious tracks were sulky acoustic guitar ballads, and let me tell ya: "The Ghost of You and Me" holds up. None of this explains why they were always dressed like Oasis. Or why they haven't pivoted to country music, because "Back Here" could use some twang.

WERE THEY A ONE-HIT WONDER? Honestly? Yes. They had some minor hits—and the Disney connection granted them decent sync deals and a guest role on the teen TV show *Even Stevens*—but "Back Here" and its addictive chorus, "Until you're back here baby / Miss you want you need you so," is the only track in their discography that will bring you back to 2000, when everything was less complicated and the US was months away from learning George W. Bush, and not "inventor of the internet" Al Gore, would become president. Yikes.

WESTLIFE (1998–2011, 2018–?)

They began as so many bad bands do, except
they weren't bad: Mark Feehily, Kian Egan, and
Shane Filan met in college in Northwest Ireland. After
performing *Grease* in their school's theater production,
they combined their talents and formed a vocal group. A few name
changes and member swaps later (the addition of Nicky Byrne and
Bryan McFadden, and the firing of a few vocalists at the wish of
Simon Cowell, who infamously said of the original lineup: "They
have great voices, but they are the ugliest band I have ever seen
in my life"), and Westlife came into existence. Boyzone manager
Louis Walsh, bewitched by the group, took over as their money
man and hooked them up with a gig opening for Backstreet Boys.
As Georgina Gregory points out in *Boy Bands and the Performance
of Pop Masculinity*, Walsh used Westlife to create something of
a master class in balancing national identity with international
consumerism: they wore department store menswear that allowed
them to fully embody a generic, apolitical, boy-next-door appearance for both Irish moms and their daughters to become infatuated
with. His scheme managed to make them the best-selling boy band
Ireland has ever seen and allowed Westlife to serve as a welcome
respite following the ethno-nationalist conflict that plagued
Northern Ireland until the end of the decade.

> WERE THEY A ONE-HIT WONDER? Definitely not! They're one of the
> most popular groups to ever come out of Ireland. End of story.

THE INTERNATIONAL BOY BAND EXPLOSION: THERE'S A BIG WORLD OUT THERE

The desire to dance and maybe even tongue-kiss a sensitive singing boy in a band who offers a delicate *je ne sais quoi* you can't get out of Luis in math class doesn't stop at the border or the Atlantic Ocean. Think of it like the hundredth monkey effect: when an idea or behavior or theory or tool surfaces in one part of the world, it simultaneously happens in another, and the knowledge spreads with incredible, unexplainable speed. Today, that's

simply called "great minds think alike" or "the internet," but in the late 1980s and 1990s, it was the consciousness-widening phenomenon known as boy bands. They were pandemic.

Describing every hunky group across the globe is a hopeless task, so here are a few of my favorites and recent discoveries worth your time and Spotify playlist.

AWAZ

Boy band Awaz, whose name is the Urdu word for "voice," formed in 1992 in Islamabad, Pakistan, where they quickly became known as the "Pakistani version of Take That." The trio—Haroon Rashid, Faakhir Mehmood, and Asad Ahmed—exploded onto the scene and released two albums before declining in popularity right at the five-year mark, in 1997, but not before their song "Janeman" became the first-ever Urdu/Hindi pop song to air on MTV Asia on April 20, 1992. They broke up in 2000.

IVANUSHKI INTERNATIONAL

In the 1980s, while Russia underwent perestroika, the country's youth began to embrace US and Western culture. By the start of the 1990s, they were fully on board with the whole boy band thing. No act was more popular than the Backstreet Boys–worshipping trio Ivanushki International (in Russian, Иванушки International), which formed in 1995. They were incredibly saturnine and romantic, and they played keytar, an underrated leftover from the '80s. (Neon synthesizers worn crossbody like the gaudiest big link chain necklace should return in the next big boy band craze. I await in leg warmers.) The group is still active but took a break in 1998, when its lead lyric writer and one of its founding members, Igor Sorin, died tragically by suicide.

MAGNETO

Not to be mistaken for the magnet man in the X-Men franchise, Magneto was a Latin-pop quintet from Mexico in the '80s and '90s who changed members so quickly, I wouldn't despise you for confusing them with Menudo. Listen to their 1991 hit "Vuela Vuela" right now if you haven't already. It's much better than the original French version, recorded in 1986 by Desireless. The '80s synth might evoke images of geometric-print sweaters and Pat Benatar headbands within you, but since when has that ever been a bad thing?

SON BY FOUR

Menudo wasn't the only boy band to call Puerto Rico home. A lot of talent resides in that tiny, 3,500-square-mile island in the Caribbean. In 1997, Son by Four took over Latin radio with their unique, modern spin on salsa and merengue, as led by Panamanian producer Omar Alfanno. The boys, brothers Javier and George Montes, Ángel López, and Pedro Quiles, hit the Billboard Hot 100 in 2000 with the English version of their single "Purest of Pain (A Puro Dolor)."

UNKNOWN TO NO ONE (UTN1)

Despite having the most badass boy band name of all time ever (Unknown to No One is, like, up there with Nine Inch Nails or Insane Clown Posse, depending on what you personally find tough and cool), this Iraqi boy band–turned–man band beat the odds. They formed in 1999 in Baghdad, under Saddam Hussein's rule, when it was dangerous to do so and many musicians had fled the country, fearing war. They also adopted Western boy band song structure and sang in both Arabic and English, which makes for some really interesting soft rock piano ballads.

CHAPTER FIVE

IT'S GONNA BE ME: *NSYNC

IN 1995, TWO years after Lou Pearlman formed the Backstreet Boys and a few more years before they'd eventually part ways, the con man had an ingenious idea: one boy band could make you wealthy, but two competing acts? That's the stuff of pop mythology. As Pearlman once told *New Yorker* journalist John Seabrook, "Where there's Coke, there's Pepsi. Someone's going to come along and do the Backstreet Boys' knockoff, so why shouldn't it be us?"

The origins of *NSYNC are contested across memoirs, documentaries, and interviews, so allow me to walk you through the most publicized turn of events. When a pint-size, musical-theater-loving child of a broken home named Chris Kirkpatrick just missed the cutoff for Backstreet Boys, he approached Pearlman, who offered him an ultimatum: find other talented, dreamboat boys, and he'd financially back another boy band. Pearlman frequently caught Kirkpatrick's performances singing a cappella doo-wop as part of the Hollywood Hi-Tones in front of Mel's Drive-In at Universal Studios Florida, but one kid does not a boy band make. Lou suggested pageant pro Justin Timberlake and star dancer Joshua "JC" Chasez of Walt Disney's *The All-New Mickey Mouse Club* to join the incipient group. (Joshua became JC professionally because there was already a Josh on *The All-New Mickey Mouse Club*. He left the show in 1995 but kept the nickname.) One alternative history suggests that Chris, not Lou, approached JC. He had been working on a record with Justin, and Kirkpatrick asked both boys join the then-nonexistent project. Another proposes that Chris and Joey called Justin about joining an a cappella ensemble. However it happened, they were now a trio. Every tale seems to include Kirkpatrick calling up his friend Joseph "Joey" Fatone Jr., whom he worked with at Universal Studios, to see if he had any interest in auditioning. Joey played the Wolfman at Beetlejuice's Rock and Roll Graveyard Revue, which is every bit as insane as the name suggests. It was also the perfect role for Joey's goofy, perpetual-party boy personality. After Lou watched his set at the theme park, he invited Fatone to join the group. Now, in desperate need for a bass vocalist and final member, Fatone asked his former classmate Jason Galasso if he'd like to join. After performing one song as a unit, he was in.

Within a few months, *NSYNC became a band, the name taken from a comment Justin Timberlake's mom, Lynn Harless, made about their talent, something along the lines of, "Man, you guys sound really in sync." The spelling was a direct reflection of their names, too: Jaso**N**, Chri**S**, Joe**Y**, Justi**N**, and **JC**, an Easter egg for fans to crack long before Taylor Swift would use hidden messages to market new album cycles. Weeks after joining, and right before signing an official contract with Pearlman's Trans Continental Records, Galasso decided to leave the boy band. He claimed he never wanted to be a teen pop idol, and so he was replaced

JUSTIN

by sixteen-year-old Mississippi blond Lance Bass, dubbed "Lansten" so they could maintain the group name. The country-music-loving, two-left-feet-possessing Bass was introduced to the group through Justin Timberlake's vocal coach Bob Westbrook back in JT's hometown of Memphis, Tennessee. (JT's mom had to convince Bass's mom to let him try out over a long afternoon of back-to-back phone calls. The rest is history, and the best case for helicopter parenting I've ever heard.) Finally, *NSYNC had its foundation and a teenager who could hit a low F.

Pearlman purchased a home for the boys in Orlando, where they resided, dormitory style, and rehearsed. He was fully in control of their lives and worked them hard so they could debut within the year. Their first live showcase was on October 20, 1995, nineteen days after Lance joined the group, at the since-shuttered Pleasure Island in Downtown Disney. Prior to the set, JT's mom compiled all of the return addresses from fan mail sent to Justin and JC in their *Mickey Mouse Club* days and invited those fans to check out their new group. Her tactic worked: a few hundred people showed up, and *NSYNC sold out the club before anyone actually knew anything about them.

The next year, with Pearlman's aid, *NSYNC signed with Backstreet Boys manager Johnny Wright. Shortly after getting the gig, Wright shared a two-song demo with Jan Bolz, an executive at BMG Ariola Munich in Germany, which resulted in *NSYNC's first record deal. Europe was infatuated with American boy bands at the time, and if building a fan base overseas before taking over the US worked for the Backstreet Boys, why wouldn't Pearlman have the same luck twice? Bolz signed *NSYNC, but he had a few demands: he wanted Lance out of the band because the guy couldn't manage to match his feet to the beat if his dreams depended on it. (They did.) Bolz also requested *NSYNC change their name. Neither happened.

In case the parallels between the two groups aren't painfully obvious yet: Like the Backstreet Boys, *NSYNC went to Sweden to record their first tracks. Their debut single, out in the fall of 1996, "I Want You Back," did numbers in Germany, but it was their second single, "Tearin' Up My Heart," that launched the group into mega fame within continental Europe. Their self-titled debut LP hit number 1 on Germany's Offizielle chart the second day it was released. Still, they were relatively unknown stateside.

That changed when Vincent DeGiorgio, an A&R rep at RCA Records in the US, a subsidiary of BMG, caught the quintet in Budapest, Hungary. He was blown away. DeGiorgio, unlike his counterparts at the other major labels who feared there could only be one best-selling boy band at a time, believed in *NSYNC enough to sign them. It also helped that by this point in the decade, Backstreet, Hanson, and the Spice Girls managed to become pop music juggernauts, indicating that radio was becoming bubblegum-friendly again and there really was a demand for sweet, safe, sparkly songs. Having perfected their trade overseas, with both Justin's and Lance's mothers chaperoning the underage boys, *NSYNC was ready to try to make it big back home. When their debut album came out stateside in March 1998, it had four tracks that were different from the European version in an attempt to captivate a sticky US market.

At first, the record didn't make a splash. Then Disney got involved. That summer, the network prepped a live concert event to air on television with the Backstreet Boys, but because Brian Littrell was quietly undergoing heart surgery at the time, the spot was offered to *NSYNC. It proved to be their career-making moment. Their performance aired on July 18, 1998, and for six months afterward on the Disney Channel, causing their debut LP to skyrocket to number 2 in America. In one evening, the telegenic boy band had taken over the States.

And, once again, in yet another mirror of the Backstreet Boys, *NSYNC realized they weren't seeing the economic benefits of being in one of the most popular boy bands of all time. JC's uncle worked with an entertainment litigator named Helene Freeman, who he requested look over their agreement with Pearlman. According to Bass's memoir, *Out of Sync*, she declared it "the worst contract in music history" and recommended they meet with music attorney Adam Ritholz. He examined the document and learned that Trans Continental took 100 percent of *NSYNC's publishing rights, 50 percent of their record royalties, 50 percent of merchandising, and 30 percent of commission on touring revenues. Pearlman had fashioned himself a sixth member of *NSYNC, too, just as he had done with the Backstreet Boys. (Pearlman claimed to take care of *NSYNC's food, dorm, whatever they needed, and gave each boy a per diem of $35 a day.) Once the group sold over 10 million records, they were presented a check for $10,000 each. After three years of wall-to-wall work and sold-out shows, that's pennies. At the very least, it's not the lifestyle of a millionaire boy band. (Bass has said it was 15 million records and a check for $25,000, which he ripped up and threw into the air. I really hope it happened that way because the detail is too deliciously dramatic, like a scene cut straight from a Lifetime original movie.) When Justin, Lance, Joey, Chris, and JC compiled their finances to hire a team of lawyers, they realized that all

JOEY

the things they thought Pearlman had been paying out of pocket for, they, as a group, were actually financing. Their lack of payment was sold to them as "recoupment," not unlike New Edition fifteen years prior.

In 1999, the boy band decided to try to renegotiate their contract with Pearlman. It didn't work, mostly because of his greed, so they began to separate themselves from him. That plan succeeded only because of a tiny contractual loophole: if Pearlman's company Trans Continental didn't sign the group to a US label within a year of recording an album, the document was void. As you recall from a few short paragraphs ago, they were signed to BMG in Germany. Pearlman sued. Eventually *NSYNC settled, left RCA and Lou, kept Wright on, and signed with Jive Records for their sophomore release, but not after triggering a $150 million breach-of-contract lawsuit by RCA's parent company, BMG, and Trans Continental. Even before the kinks of the settlement were established, the judge gave *NSYNC permission to go ahead and release their second album, *No Strings Attached*, a title reflective of their newfound freedom post-Pearlman.

When the LP dropped in March 2000, it sold more than 1.2 million copies in its first day and over 2.4 million copies in its first week, doubling and demolishing the record set in 1999 by the Backstreet Boys' *Millennium,* and setting a world record they held for over fifteen years. (For the music chart nerds reading this: they were beat by the retro English singer-songwriter Adele, and her sophomore album, *25*, in November 2015.)

No Strings Attached gave *NSYNC their biggest single to date, the propulsive dance pop "Bye Bye Bye," complete with iconic choreography, like the bratty "talk too much" single-hand clap and partnering fist bump. *No Strings* became not only the best-selling album of 2000 and their first number 1 album, but also the best-selling album of the decade. By December 2009, it sold a whopping 10 million copies. "It's Gonna Be Me" became their first number 1 single. They scored the cover of *Rolling Stone*. In 2001, they performed during the special "The Kings of Rock and Pop" Super Bowl halftime show alongside Aerosmith, Britney Spears, Mary J. Blige, and Nelly. Justin starred in the Disney Channel original movie *Model Behavior*, my favorite film from the years 2000–2001. The boy band was asked to perform and run the torch at the 2002 Winter Olympic Games. They were officially a global success story, just not a sustainable one.

In 2001, *NSYNC released what would become their third and final album, *Celebrity*. It sold really well, 1.9 million units in a week, but produced no number 1 singles. ("Girlfriend," featuring Nelly, hit number 5.) On *Celebrity*, Justin took the lead instead of JC, the dominant voice on *No Strings* save for its singles, highlighting the group's move deeper into R&B territory and foreshadowing Timberlake's future solo successes. *NSYNC embarked on two stadium tours and then, in the spring of 2002, abruptly announced a temporary hiatus that became permanent.

No one made use of their break quite like Lance Bass, who moved to Star City, Russia, with the goal of becoming the youngest person in space. (You're not reading the plot of some hyperbolic "alternative universe" fan fiction. He really is that interesting.) He completed cosmonaut training, six months of prep for spaceflight aboard a Soyuz spacecraft, for a documentary that never saw the light

CHRIS

of day. Bass never made it to the final frontier, either, but he did become an advocate for its exploration and was nicknamed "Lance Basstronaut" by the press. There are more photographs of him preparing to take off than of the band in *Out of Sync*, which I only mention now because it is hilarious and I really do hope he makes it to space someday.

The boy band regrouped infrequently during their break, and they held a final, private meeting in the summer of 2004 to discuss future aspirations. It was there that Justin Timberlake, arguably the biggest star to come out of the boy band machine, announced his departure from the group and desire to go solo. "I was growing out of it," Timberlake reflected on his decision in a 2017 interview with the *Hollywood Reporter*. "I felt like I cared more about the music than some of the other people in the group. And I felt like I had other music I wanted to make and that I needed to follow my heart."

His departure altered the model of how boy bands could behave. Now, because of Justin, you could voluntarily leave your boy band and have a career that eclipses the group that made you, as long as you appeal to your loyal pop audience and alter your sound enough to appeal to the growing adult interest, too. You're getting older, and your fans are as well. There's no use in pretending otherwise.

If JT's exit wasn't enough confirmation that the boy band was confirmed dead on arrival, the release of a greatest hits album in 2005 etched their epitaph. They hung up their impossibly small tinted sunglasses and matching iridescent snowsuits for good. But like the proverbial phoenix, a star was reborn from the ashes. And his name was Justin.

*NSYNC
VS.
THE BACKSTREET BOYS

IN NOVEMBER 1998, Johnny Wright told *Rolling Stone* he, Donna Wright, and Pearlman would joke that they were "going to turn Orlando into the next Motown, but we were going to call it Snowtown—because we weren't doing it with R&B acts, we were doing it with pop acts. I guess you could say Backstreet Boys are the Temptations and *NSYNC are the Four Tops." A more accurate comparison would be the Beatles vs. the Rolling Stones. You loved and identified with one or the other, never both. That would be a cop-out. At any rate, they were two different beasts: the Backstreet Boys focused on harmonies, wore dark colors, and were all-around moodier. *NSYNC were seen as the boys next door in jerseys, shorts, and Jordans, the guys who placed the most value on live performance.

Similar to how New Kids on the Block never publicly expressed animosity toward New Edition, whose style they essentially stole, *NSYNC never really felt any bad blood toward the Backstreet Boys. Understandably, that didn't go both ways. (For what it's worth, *NSYNC was intimidated by the Backstreet Boys—at least, by what the Boys might do to them if they were to ever cross paths. It was a real *West Side Story* situation.) To the Backstreet Boys, *NSYNC was created by the man that made their dreams come true to destroy them. "It's not *NSYNC itself but where *NSYNC comes from that digs me, digs me, digs me and gets me, still and to this day," Backstreet Boys' Kevin Richardson told *Rolling Stone* in 2000. "Mr. Pearlman was always speaking loyalty and preaching loyalty, saying, 'I love you guys; you're like my sons.' And I'd lost my father to cancer. So, I looked at Lou like a father figure. But I was naïve, and he's a liar. We'll always remember him for helping us get started. But we'll also remember him for screwing us blind and building another group behind our backs."

Regardless of the boy bands' common enemy, their fabricated rivalry was the stuff of marketing dreams. Contemporary acts with similar success on near-identical paths would be perceived as enemies forevermore: In the solo artist space, Britney Spears and Christina Aguilera duked it out. In One Direction's earliest stages, English band the Wanted—a much, much smaller act, but one with a dedicated, loyal, and organized fan base online—was pitted against them. Backstreet and *NSYNC might've felt uncomfortable with each other, but their true hatred was reserved for the man they also owed a lot to: Pearlman.

Conspiracy Corner:
Chris Kirkpatrick
vs. AJ McLean

LIKE ANY INSTANCE of public friction, there are many conspiracy theories tied to the great *NSYNC vs. Backstreet Boys debate. And because boy band appreciation is a peculiar passion you never fully grow out of, these hypotheses continue to arise whenever boy bands go on reunion tours and journalists dig up old dirt like kleptomaniac magpies. (I can say that. I am one.) Case in point: in 2018, *NSYNC's Chris Kirkpatrick told *Billboard* that though he believes his band is only guilty of creating friendly competition between acts, he also wanted "to punch AJ [McLean]'s lights out for a little while." Apparently Kirkpatrick was dating a girl, broke up with her, and she started dating the Backstreet Boy. He said, "I guess he was talking smack to her about me, so I confronted him on it and wanted to kick his ass." He added, "I think boy band fights are in the same realm as hockey fights. You fight when you're on TV . . . Now we're really good friends."

Could it be that the real source of antagonism was not because of each other's success or Pearlman, but over a woman? If they were more popular members of each band fighting over a date, like Nick Carter and Justin Timberlake, surely the press would've covered it more back then? And who was she?

RECOGNIZING THE PANDEMONIUM Backstreet and *NSYNC inspired, MTV, then the definitive arbiter of youth culture, sought to monetize the countless music video requests they received from eager boy band fans. In 1998, they found their *Soul Train*, their *American Bandstand*, their *Top of the Pops*, and most significantly, their solution: *Total Request Live*. *TRL*, which first hit the air on September 14, 1998, was innovative. It was interactive television like nothing pop culture programming had seen before, high but not surprising praise for the landmark network in its own adolescence (MTV debuted in 1981).

Before *TRL* there was *Dial MTV*, MTV's first music video request show, which splintered off into two short-lived late '90s incarnations: *Total Request*, essentially the same concept hosted by Carson Daly, and *MTV Live*, a live show that incorporated performances and real-time artist interviews. Realizing that those programs could and absolutely should have been merged into one, *TRL*, hosted by Daly, became both: a real-time top-ten video countdown show complete with artist interviews and concerts. The live aspect gave it a no-holds-barred freedom young people desired (though MTV ultimately controlled the pool of music fans could choose from and vote on), and the ranked video system required popular acts to interact with each other in unpredictable ways. Not to mention, *TRL* turned kids on to a variety of different music, foreshadowing the kind of genre-agnostic "I listen to everything" attitude later generations would possess.

First held in a private studio without an audience, which co-creator Bob Kusbit described to *Billboard* as being *"Wayne's World*-style," and later moved to its iconic 1515 Broadway address in New York City's Times Square, *TRL* was an experiment blessed by perfect timing. The music industry had never seen the kind of sales boy bands and teen pop stars were raking in, and fans sought access to the epic personalities behind them. *TRL* gave them exactly that, from 3:30 to 4:30 p.m. EST each weekday, a perfect ritual that hit right after school. For those lucky enough to flood the street during its filming, the studio's windowed walls allowed fans to wave, scream, and make homemade signs to grab the attention of their favorite musician without having to wait for a new tour date to come to town. Picture the *Today* show, but for people with nose studs.

Without *TRL*, it's hard to imagine that the Backstreet Boys and *NSYNC (and LFO, and O-Town, and all the other boy bands) would've had the far-ranging appeal they did. JC Chasez referred to it as a symbiotic relationship, and that might be the most astute way of describing it. Boy bands of this era understood that kids had the power to alter the framework of popular music by being the largest consumers of it, and *TRL* gave them a place to voice their musical opinions. It bred competition between acts, helped keep boy band videos in rotation atop the chart, and more or less fathered the nu-metal musical movement that opposed the boy band craze: hard rock acts like Korn, who are gross, macho, mean, and manly, the opposite of Nick Carter. Without Pearlman's groups, there would be no Limp Bizkit for the boys who hated boy bands to rally behind. What a sad world that would be.

Style Watch: Blue Jean Dreaming

THE YEAR: 2001. The event: the American Music Awards. Faith Hill will take home the most trophies, followed closely by Toni Braxton and Christian arena rockers Creed. Kid Rock has yet to make incredulous comments in support of Donald Trump and will be awarded handsomely for his contributions to society (as far as I can tell, it is exclusively giving twelve-year-old boys everywhere the testosterone-dripping, incoherent chorus of "Badwitdaba da bang da bang diggy diggy diggy"). Beyoncé is known only as the best voice in Destiny's Child. (Down is up?) And Britney Spears, with longtime beau Justin Timberlake, will wear one of the most memorable red carpet looks of all time, topped only by Bjork's swan dress at the Academy Awards two months later. A pop-culture-loving society, so emboldened by our new lives in the twenty-first century as survivors of the Y2K scare, could take on anything. And so, the greatest pop power couple of the early '00s took on jeans.

The thought process seems linear enough: If denim isn't traditionally formalwear, why is denim-on-denim called a Canadian tuxedo? If the girl group Dream is going to show up in impossibly low-rise flare jeans, grommet belts, and distressed baby tees, why not elevate trends into immortality? And so, Britney and Justin did just that, in matching denim looks boasting of details remarkably *them*: for Justin, the good ol' Shelby Forest, Tennessee boy with dreamy pipes and high hopes that led him to the cultural

hub of Orlando, Florida, a cowboy hat. For Ms. Spears, a glamorously thick diamond choker and matching bracelet, a patchwork denim gown with a bustier and matching purse for her L.A. via LA—that is, Los Angeles via Louisiana—hometown appeal. It was instantly infamous, impressively bad fashion in a time where all trends were unflattering. (Try to picture the Von Dutch trucker hats, heeled Timberlands, skirts over flared pants, and other various travesties the world has collectively repressed.) JT and Brit's style was unmissable, embellished Americana, a look that played to the award show's identity, to their own, and to the fantasy of millions watching at home. What's more relatable than jeans? What's more Hollywood than jeans you and I could never pull off? Or afford?

In 2013, Spears told MTV the matching outfits were her idea. Considering that JT's far-too-hair-sprayed hair, which closely resembled dry ramen noodles, was covered with a hat, and that her middle name is literally Jean, it's feasible. At the very least, it marked a moment: Justin and Britney broke up a year later, in 2002 (coincidentally when *NSYNC went on hiatus) after a few years of dating in the public eye. They'd known each other since they were kids in puppy love on Disney's *All-New Mickey Mouse Club* and eventually gave each other their first kiss and probably that v-card swipe, two things boy band fans did not want to know about, but at the same time were deeply invested in. Such is the cognitive dissonance of the boy band fan. The matching ensemble only served to highlight Justin and Britney's apparent dedication to one another, but as fans learned, all that glitters isn't Levi's.

When Timberlake paid Australian talk show *The Project* a visit in 2016 and was hit with "What have you learned about the industry that you didn't know when you were in *NSYNC that you know now?" he answered, "If you wear denim-on-denim, it will get documented…I don't even think I could bring that back." That same year, Britney's denim dress was sold at auction for $7,199. Experts (me) theorize Timberlake's suit was destroyed after wear or is sitting in a Plexiglas case in the far corner of a Hard Rock Cafe somewhere. That's known as celebrity fashion purgatory.

Much of the growth process for a solo musician post–boy band is learning to individuate, to separate himself from his youthful indiscretions. Timberlake's dismissal of a style that has since been embraced as iconic shouldn't come as a surprise; no one deserves to be questioned about all the weird stuff they wore at age twenty for the next twenty years. Nonetheless, its enduring legacy speaks to a generation's total obsession. The denim outfits are the image of their relationship, one that signifies the beginning of the end: of Justin and Britney, and of *NSYNC, too.

BOYS IN THE BAND WHO LOVE BOYS

Boy bands' acceptance of all people—specifically that of the LGBTQIA+ community—is integral to their message of inclusion and a driving force for their success. It should come as no surprise, then, that a handful of boy band members past and present have come out as gay: New Kids on the Block's Jonathan Knight, Menudo's Ricky Martin, Westlife's Markus Feehily, Boyzone's Stephen Gately, and *NSYNC's Lance Bass, to name a few.

As common as it is for boy bands to have gay members, it's also assumed that they won't reveal their sexuality until after the boy band has broken up or is winding down. As Bass told *The Rubin Report* in 2013, "You have the record labels and everyone grooming you to make sure you don't even mention you have a girlfriend. So, screw the fact that you are going to come out as being gay. It ruins their whole business plan." Boyzone, happily, challenged expectation. As Gately told the *Sunday Times Magazine* when he opened up about having a male partner in 1999, "I desperately wanted to be a pop star but decided early on I couldn't do that and be gay. I had to keep it to myself. Being honest would mean saying goodbye to fame. Knowing that [the band] understood and supported me helped me with the pressure that was building up." He began dating Eloy de Jong of Dutch boy band Caught in the Act, and Boyzone welcomed a new, large, passionate queer fan base immediately after he announced his sexuality publicly. Surely this signals another change in the boy band design: there's power in owning your queerness.

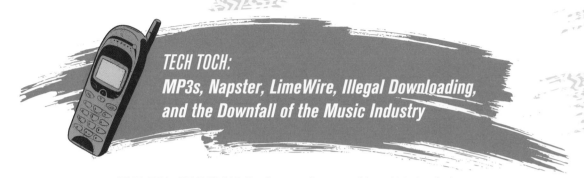

THE ERA OF *NSYNC, Backstreet Boys, and late '90s/early '00s teen pop as a whole was by far the best-selling time in music business history. Period. People spent money on music ownership whatever the cost, and it was not cheap. In 2000, compact discs ran about $13–$20 and even more in the UK, averaging £17, or $23–$25 per CD, depending on the exchange rate. Kids with access to their parents' disposable income bought multiple albums a week when something tells me the couple hundo families shelled out at Best Buy or Tower Records every few months could've gone to the mortgage in an ever-inflating housing market.

Say you heard "Larger Than Life" on the radio, muttered, "Hey! That has a funky groove," and decided you must have it. In 1999, there was no way to purchase the sole song, no affordable single-format device à la the cassingle. You'd have to spend nearly $20 on an album full of insipid moments to own the three minutes and forty-three seconds of pop perfection. The music industry was impelling its consumers to spend money on crap they didn't even want (in the case of *Millennium*, ten tracks of near-filler, and I say that as someone who holds the album close to her heart). Clearly, the model was unviable and a bubble was going to burst.

It did, and hard. As soon as both BSB and *NSYNC kicked the bucket, illegal digital music services like Napster, LimeWire, and Kazaa took over, and the music industry collapsed. It would never recover, even with the growing success of legal streaming services like Spotify and Apple Music in the '10s.

Consumer discontent best explains the giant shift in the business that followed. With the advent of the MP3, Winamp, iTunes, early digital music libraries that supplanted the place of clunky CD binders, and the growth of the previously mentioned illegal file-sharing services, paying to own music (expensive) became a thing of the past (free). As Steve Knopper wrote in his 2009 book, *Appetite for Self-Destruction: The Spectacular Crash of the Record Industry in the Digital Age*, "It was no coincidence…that Napster, the free file-sharing service, popped up on the internet at precisely this time. The least frustrating way to obtain 'I Want It That Way' in 1999 or 2000 was to download it for free. Illegally." And you wouldn't have to waste time on the whole album if you didn't want to, either. Singles were back.

Not only did digital music services allow fans to acquire, copy, and distribute their favorite songs illegally, it also introduced them to an eclectic mix of genres previously inaccessible. (Unless you had a cool older sister in college in New York, and she worked at a cool record store like Other Music and had an affinity for cool international sounds. Most of us aren't so lucky. Or cool.) Because of the technologies and downloading platforms cropping up, listenership broadened beyond whatever aired on *TRL*. By introducing new sounds and new competition to impressionable audiences, and due to the fact that fans were no longer purchasing the music they enjoyed, success through sales alone became a thing of the past. Boy bands, however, would never die. They just had to get creative.

HIT CLIPS

The *NSYNC/Backstreet Boys epoch coincided with the invention of Hit Clips, launched by Hasbro's Tiger Electronics in 1999. They were tiny, portable music playing devices in which USB-like disc chips were inserted into keychain-size players, described as "slick micro audio systems" in the alarmingly Y2K-era commercials. Because it was early toy technology, each disc only played about one minute of a single hit song, long enough for the chorus and the hook. Their size made them ripe for collection and cooler than a charm bracelet. Tweens with the greatest cultural clout attached their Hit Clips to the zipper of their teal Jansport backpacks, next to their miniature Beanie Babies key ring, a colorful knickknack distracting from the Game Boy Color that lay within. (Children of the late '90s know what I'm talking about.)

As time went on, the shape of Hit Clips changed from Walkman-like to mini boom boxes and CD players. Each Hit Clip system ran about $20, and each disc was about $3.99—and remember, they weren't even full songs! That's an exorbitant cost for something that runs the risk of total destruction every time the school bus driver decides to take a speed bump with some torque. Hit Clips were also proto-iPod, which was introduced two years later, in 2001, and became the standard for mobile listening.

While the sound quality wasn't anything to write home about, Hit Clips were still incontestably adorable and the talk of the town for the sixteen-and-under crowd, Tamagotchi style. I miss them every day.

CHAPTER SIX

BURNIN' UP: THE JONAS BROTHERS

NOT FAR FROM the New York City skyline and, on a good day, about an hour drive away sits Wyckoff, New Jersey, a predominantly middle-class, predominantly white, predominantly Republican sleepy suburb. In the early 2000s, the Garden town in the Garden State, as its Dutch settlers referred to it, is where brothers Nick, Joe, and Kevin Jonas could be found attending sermons given by their father, Kevin Jonas Sr., a pastor at the local Assembly of God church. The boys grew up performing music in their house of worship, which in turn inspired them to start their own band. The Jonas Brothers, formerly known as J3, came into existence in 2005, when its youngest and most prodigious member, Nick, was twelve years old—a year after he signed a solo deal with Columbia Records. Before the JoBros formed, each brother found himself auditioning and actually landing gigs acting in prominent commercials and plays, including *Les Misérables* and *La Bohème* on Broadway. Nick, then known as Nicholas, released a self-titled Christian-tinted pop-rock record in early 2005, but the execs at his major label had their eyes set on a secular boy band of brothers with undeniable creative chemistry. (Shouldn't each era get the Hanson it deserves?) I mean, *come on*, they all had unignorably bodacious brunette curls, and good hair is as much of a prerequisite as the ability to harmonize. In 2006, the JoBros released their debut album, *It's About Time*. It didn't hit, despite the fact that the single "Mandy" and its lyrics—"Mandy used to be that girl / The one that never said a word / But she always sang / S Club 7 and all those boy bands"—are timeless. The next year, the band was dropped by Columbia.

The combination of *NSYNC and Backstreet Boys embarking on indefinite hiatuses in 2002, the explosion of illegal file sharing, and the growing popularity of other musical styles meant that for the first half of the '00s, there were no boy bands. (And if you're asking yourself, "Well, what about the Click Five?" please return to chapter 2 and refamiliarize yourself with the qualifications for boy bands; you'll see that they don't fit the format. They are a pop-rock group. I will admit "Just the Girl" holds up. You can have that.) It's only when enough time has passed that boy bands can return to the top of the charts, and the JoBros were ready to bring it back.

The music-hungry young women who fuel a boy band's audience stepped away post-Backstreet to heed the advice of MTV's *TRL*, whose programming aged them into R&B women soloists or, more linearly, pop-punk groups like Blink-182, the emo-vaudevillian stylings of Panic! at the Disco, the tight-pants-and-eyeliner-wearing Fall Out Boy, and anything else that performed well on MySpace. Since rock and roll gave the first American teenagers freedom to swing their hips in the '50s, that kind of musicianship has always had sensual appeal. Add the sensitive poetry of a pop-punk-emo musician with a broken heart, and you've all but modernized the

NICK

boy band modus operandi by a different name: a rock band. The Jonas Brothers, ever the savvy pop music fans, took notes as the teen climate changed in an attempt to salvage what appeared to be their already unraveling career. Why couldn't there be a nonthreatening pop-punk boy band? Why couldn't they be the ones to try?

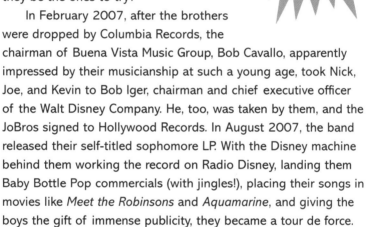

KEVIN

In February 2007, after the brothers were dropped by Columbia Records, the chairman of Buena Vista Music Group, Bob Cavallo, apparently impressed by their musicianship at such a young age, took Nick, Joe, and Kevin to Bob Iger, chairman and chief executive officer of the Walt Disney Company. He, too, was taken by them, and the JoBros signed to Hollywood Records. In August 2007, the band released their self-titled sophomore LP. With the Disney machine behind them working the record on Radio Disney, landing them Baby Bottle Pop commercials (with jingles!), placing their songs in movies like *Meet the Robinsons* and *Aquamarine*, and giving the boys the gift of immense publicity, they became a tour de force.

As of 2015, the Jonas Brothers had sold 1.9 million copies of the album. (Astonishingly, those weren't all straight to iPod Nano.) The band repurposed their cover of English pop-rock band Busted's sleeper hit "Year 3000" from their first LP for their self-titled second, where it debuted at number 40 on the Billboard Hot 100 and became their first smash. By that point, the Jonas Brothers were unstoppable. They straightened most of their curls for some rock-and-roll edge and had the pop-punk chops to prove themselves decent songwriters in their original material, singles like "S.O.S," "Hold On," and "When You Look Me in the Eyes." In August, they guest-starred on an episode of *Hannah Montana*, foreshadowing future acting work and their inescapable transition into Disney Channel stars. The JoBros embraced an intensive schedule while performing music that existed somewhere between *NSYNC and Green Day; they appealed to the popular sound at the time while managing to make it much more innocent, safer… more Disney.

In 2008, now some of the most well-known people on the planet, the Jonas Brothers released their third album and their second with Disney, *A Little Bit Longer*. It was massive Rick Springfield–cum–Vans' Warped Tour worship, and with hits like "Burnin' Up," "Lovebug," and "Tonight," the record sold over 500,000 copies in its first two months on shelves. That might not sound so spectacular when compared to the numbers Backstreet Boys were pulling in their heyday, but it is impressive when taking into account that this was the beginning of die-hard and casual fans alike realizing they didn't have to pay for music, so they simply didn't.

Regardless, the album peaked at number 1 on the Billboard 200, their first time atop the chart. Critics, clearly enraptured by the band's ability to play their own instruments and also write their own songs in contrast to other boy bands, didn't instinctively deride their music. *Rolling Stone* even named "Video Girl" one of the best songs of the year for its "uncharacteristically nasty and characteristically catchy swipe at chicks-on-the-make." Unsurprisingly, it's the most misogynistic tune in their repertoire, but one young women could listen to and visualize their lives with these boys. They wouldn't be like those "other girls," the groupies, the parasitic paramours. They're not in it for the fame and money, honey.

Disney began to realize the boys had real acting ability—after all, that is how their showbiz careers began—so the conglomerate workshopped ways in which the Jonas Brothers' musical star power could traffic eyeballs over to their television network. In Hollywood, that's called synergy. The JoBros portrayed themselves in a few short-lived docuseries called *Jonas Brothers: Living the Dream*, *Jonas Brothers: Live in London*, *Jonas Brothers: Band in a Bus*, *Jonas Brothers: Live and Mobile*, and probably a few more I've forgotten, but their silver screen moment arrived in the summer of 2008, when most school-aged kids were home for the season and available to binge watch the Disney Channel, in a film called *Camp Rock*. Joe was the star.

JOE

At that point in time, the Disney Channel had a long history of releasing movies straight to cable. They aired with such regularity that they quickly became cult classics for indoor kids who may find themselves watching from the comfort of an air-conditioned room in the dead of June. The corporation had an inimitable ability to tell coming-of-age stories partnered with big pop songs sung by prominent people in their network. So, when the JoBros landed the role of Connect 3 (a pop-rock boy band of brothers, go figure) alongside rising starlet Demi Lovato for a G-rated summertime camp movie, it was guaranteed to be a hit. And it was, generating enough demand for a second film, 2010's *Camp Rock 2: The Final Jam*. In the midst of all that, the Jonas Brothers starred in their own Disney Channel television show called *Jonas* for two seasons, where they played characters named Kevin, Joe, and Nick Lucas, members of a best-selling boy band who also attended high school. Now fully famous and fully adults, the once-compliant trio began to question how strange it was that a then twenty-year-old Joe Jonas was forced to shave multiple times a day to appear sixteen on the show when he was pushing the legal drinking age. *Jonas* was for children, and they no longer were. In their 2019 Amazon documentary *Chasing Happiness*, Nick says the second season of *Jonas* is his biggest regret with the band. "It really stunted our growth," he deadpans to Joe and Kevin. "Literally, we couldn't evolve because of it."

Amid films, tours, and a Grammy nomination (definitely unheard-of territory for a '00s boy band that was mostly ignored by prestige institutions), the Jonas Brothers released their fourth album, 2009's *Lines, Vines and Trying Times*. The record didn't produce any hits quite as large as those on the last two, but it still debuted at number 1. In retrospect, the title was telling, and in 2013, the Jonas Brothers announced their indefinite hiatus on *Good Morning America*. When they reunited in 2019, the band revealed Nick Jonas was mainly to blame for the breakup. He wanted to pursue music as a solo artist, which proved to be very successful for him. (For what it's worth, he was also the architect of the reunion. Forgive him.) In that time, Joe would release a flop of a solo album, 2011's *Fastlife*, before forming another dance-y pop-rock band, DNCE, and Kevin would star in an E! celebrity television show, *Married to Jonas*.

The trio's 2019 comeback track, "Sucker," became their first number 1 single on the Billboard Hot 100, proving that with the perfect combination of nostalgia, continued relevancy, loyal fandom, and musical talent, boy band influence ain't nothing to fuck with.

IT'S ABOUT PURITY RINGS

The Jonas Brothers' ascent from New Jersey pop-punkers to bona fide, Disney-backed boy band perfectly overlapped with an ongoing shift in popular culture known as the purity movement. After Justin Timberlake and his contemporaries Britney Spears and Christina Aguilera aged out of the kid-friendly network, they began to explore their sexuality publicly (the *NSYNC front man's 2002 solo debut, *Justified*, was riddled with innuendo). Unable to compete, Disney needed to establish a new generation ready to push forward an agenda of chastity. As writer Hazel Cills points out for Jezebel, there were political motivations for this: President George W. Bush's Community-Based Abstinence Education Program gave federal funding to abstinence-based (and faith-based) sex education organizations as a means to curb teen pregnancy rates, presumably choosing to ignore all the science that has proven celibacy-focused indoctrination to be ineffective. (President Barack Obama rolled back those measures in 2010, coincidentally, the same year the Jonas Brothers performed at the White House.) This change, and JT's move toward sexy mainstream music, left Disney with a big space to fill, music that would please parents and a conservative government at the same time. And so they created their own Christian, virgin, purity-ring-toting roster of young, impressionable pop stars: Hilary Duff, Selena Gomez, Demi Lovato, Miley Cyrus, and the Jonas Brothers.

The JoBros were the ideal poster children for the movement. It didn't hurt that when they were around ten or eleven years old, they signed up for a religious program called True Love Waits; rocking a purity ring was an extension of their childhood decision to wait for marriage. As cute young boys and the sons of a pastor, no less, they drew in a young female fan base undergoing their own sexual awakening. Since they wore purity rings as literal symbols of virginity, the memo was clear: to get with us, you better be pure. Family values and evangelical Christianity were one and the same in the early '00s tweendom, and these young pop stars and television actors wore rings to prove it. (In fact, the Jonas Brothers even sold replicas of Nick Jonas's purity ring, which included an engraving of the extremely embarrassing '00s slang word "PONED.") Indubitably, that kind of thinly veiled moral and ethical posturing was dangerous for young women. Having sex as a teenager doesn't make you a slut or less than, and purity rings' religious exclusivity all but shouted that coded sexism from the rooftops. Think about it: this was when feminism was vintage Spice Girls' corporatized girl power and little else. It was not the most radical time to be a girl.

In the press, with hindsight being 20/20, the Jonas Brothers have claimed that they never meant for their purity ring wearing to become that much of a thing. Or anything at all. Joe has said in multiple interviews that his band only agreed to wear the rings when they were young and unaware of the jewelry's full weight or how they would feel about it come adolescence. The band only spoke about it when an interviewer gave them an ultimatum: explain the rings, or he was going to make something up about a cult affiliation. Out of fear, they told the truth, and it reverberated, hard.

Eventually the Jonas Brothers (and Duff, Gomez, Lovato, and Cyrus) would remove their rings. Kevin Jonas was first, unsurprising since he married in 2009 at twenty-one years old, and later Nick and Joe did the same, as they moved to their late teens and grew more and more interested in the opposite sex. Neither boy actually waited for marriage, but an obsession with purity and the Jonas Brothers as the ultimate symbol of Christian repression continued. *South Park*, the crude, inexplicably popular animated

television show, dedicated an entire episode to the Jonas Brothers and their purity rings, complete with a parody performance of their hit single "Burnin' Up." (The opening lyrics became "I'm ready / To get it on / But there's no gettin' on / Till I'm ready / It's too soon / Slow down.") The joke was that by wearing the purity rings, the Jonas Brothers could effectively sell sex to teenage girls without making it as transparent as the openly sensual pop music on the radio, and that teen girls, Disney fans, Christians, and anyone else involved with the purity movement were idiots. Something tells me *The Simpsons* would've done a more delicate job. There's no way Lisa wasn't a Jonas Brothers fan. No precocious eight-year-old of a certain time could be immune to their magnetism.

Then, like Justin Timberlake, Britney Spears, and the other Disney stars before them, the Jonas Brothers dove into the deep end of expressing their sexuality, sans vulgarity. If you're envisioning stereotypes of lapsed Christians turning into total thots in their twenties and partying up a storm, you're right on the money. Unlike JT, who rumor has it told one of Spears's choreographers, Darrin Henson, "Dude, smell my fingers…Just slept with her that night," a year into their relationship, the JoBros left their sexual proclivities to the imagination. Joe Jonas has been the most revealing, telling queer publication *Pride Source* in 2016, when he was twenty-seven, "I feel like I'm free in my life to speak about [sex], and yeah, everyone should try a little bit of something new in the bedroom. It's definitely fun when you bring some whips and leather and whatever you may be into—a little bit of S&M." In retrospect, the BDSM comment seems to allude to his role in the 2019 "Sucker" music video, where his wife licks her lips while examining Joe, who's tied up in rope bondage, shibari style. Someone clearly watched *Fifty Shades of Grey* and likes to be dommed.

For each member, the loss of virginity and the removal of the purity ring opened the floodgates for healthy conversation about sexuality that wasn't so damn repressive and regressive. Nick told *Elle* in 2015, "There was so much attention on my sex life at 15. It was uncomfortable. If you were talking about a 15-year-old's sex life…in any other context it would be totally obscene," he continued. "[The purity ring] shaped my view of the importance of sex…It was about me being comfortable with my decisions. As a 22-year-old man, I'm a man in all ways, and I'm comfortable with that. It's freeing now to be transparent."

Luckily for JoBro fans, they were able to grow up with the band and remove their metaphorical rings as well. Hopefully, they, too, were able to develop a more mature and progressive relationship with their libidinal desires.

Style Watch

BOY BAND FASHION is only as good as the fads of the decade each group comes up in, so who could really blame the Jonas Brothers for their hideously mid-'00s looks? Much like their music, the style of the JoBros themselves is best described as the physical manifestation of the *Tony Hawk's Underground* soundtrack, or Hot Topic. All of their fashion could be purchased at the mall, which isn't a bad thing. It isn't a great thing, either, especially when the most daring trend of the time was called "guyliner" and describing people as "metrosexual" was in vogue. Of the three bros, Joe Jonas was the most daring in his contemporary style, so let's use him as the example.

*   In the early Jonas Brothers days, the boys were adored for their curly locks. As they progressed on to the Disney Channel, only Nick kept his natural, boyish ringlets pristine. Joe straightened his hair to the point where it would obstruct his vision. At the time, there was nothing sexier than optical irritation. Pop-punk kids and literary teens in the suburbs keep the haircut alive, and I love them for it.

*   In true angsty rock-and-roll fashion, Joe always wore buttons and a skinny tie, edgy embellishments to classic menswear. He was a punk, and so was his tiny vest. Can I make it any more obvious?

*   Virgin, tattooless skin hid beneath Joe's tighter-than-a-girl's-grip-on-the-barricade-front-row-at-a-Jonas-Brothers-concert black skinny jeans. Both were crucial aspects of his overall "I can protect you, but also I can't lift a twin amp" vibe.

*   Only two pairs of shoes existed for the Jonas Brothers: Converse Chuck Taylors or Vans slip-ons, customarily with a checkerboard pattern. That's convenient, because both shoes were affordable and readily available at Journeys, next door to PacSun.

FLAT-IRONED HAIR FOR DECREASED VISIBILITY

TOO-TIGHT SUIT FIT ADORNED WITH POP-PUNK BUTTONS

JOE JONAS

SKINNY JEANS

CHUCKS

LOVEBUG: THE JONASES AND THEIR BOGUS DATING LIVES

Since the Jonas Brothers were big into purity rings and being sweet little goody-goodies with angular haircuts, their dating pool was limited to other prim, proper, and prissy pop stars whose edginess could only be expressed through blunt bangs and studded white belts. At a time when Avril Lavigne was the pinnacle of punk, the JoBros reserved their hand-holding for other Disney Channel starlets who came up in the same evangelical regime. Oh, and Taylor Swift, who totally could've been signed to Hollywood Records, but wasn't. Her branding was similarly sanctimonious.

Of course, Kevin was always committed to his girlfriend-turned-wife Danielle Jonas (née Deleasa), but Joe and Nick got around town and their fans never recovered.* Here are a few that burned.

JOE JONAS AND AJ MICHALKA

According to *J-14*, the ultimate authority in celeb tween dating, Joe Jonas linked up with actor AJ Michalka from December 2005 through November 2006. You know her from the Disney Channel original movie *Cow Belles* and her role as one half of the sister pop vocal duo Aly & AJ. Allegedly, they met at the Cheetah Girls' Cheetah-licious Christmas tour. If that's not textbook romance, I don't know what is. Fans seem to think that AJ wrote her biggest

---

* At least they weren't having sex?

hit, "Potential Breakup Song," about her relationship with Joe Jonas, which I really hope is true, because that song is eternal and he should feel so honored.

JOE JONAS AND TAYLOR SWIFT

Disregarding the fact that they only dated from July to October 2008, both Taylor Swift and Joe Jonas have gotten some mileage out of the fact that they were together and then were not together. They used their individual fame to make one big ol' beautiful capital-F Famous Couple, and the tween tabloids could not get enough. When Joe broke up with Taylor, he purportedly did so in a twenty-seven-second phone call, which may or may not have inspired some of Swift's most biting and brilliant songs. If only all celebriteen pairings could be so productive.

JOE JONAS AND DEMI LOVATO

There are few feelings more rewarding in the boy band fan experience (short of actually boning the object of your affection, which actually throws the power dynamic all out of whack, so it's best to keep the squishing of downstairs parts to advanced fan fiction) than watching your celebrity ships happen in real life. Here's an example: Joe Jonas was Demi Lovato's first kiss, and it happened onset of *Camp Rock*. Clearly moved by the

film as much as I was, the pair dated for a stint in 2010. They're buds even to this day, which is sweet, but not as sweet as that innocently amorous smooch.

JOE JONAS AND ASHLEY GREENE

Joe Jonas told *New York Magazine* in 2013 that he dated and lost his virginity to a vampire from *Twilight*, Alice Cullen aka Ashley Greene, when he was twenty years old. I can't imagine they were anyone's favorite ship, but you have to respect the youth-centric cross-promotion. Sources could not confirm if any blood sucking was involved.

JOE JONAS AND GIGI HADID

Long before Zayn Malik from One Direction and Gigi Hadid shacked up, and only partially before the Kardashians took over popular culture and determined that supermodels were cool again, Joe and Gigi were an item. Joe even made a few appearances on *The Real Housewives of Beverly Hills* because Gigi's mom, Yolanda Hadid, was featured on the program (the ultimate famous boyfriend sacrifice, in my humble opinion). That was long after the JoBros had called it quits, but Joe was cuter than ever, fully rocking his new band DNCE, and improbably talented at keeping up his own relevancy.

NICK JONAS AND MILEY CYRUS

It wouldn't be right to say Nick Jonas was a bit more discerning with his dating history, because slut-shaming anyone, including boy bands, sucks. As the youngest of the group, he wasn't playing tonsil hockey with any of his fellow Disney Channel mates until he met a young Miley Cyrus and wrote "Wedding Bells" about her.

They dated in 2006 and ended things in late 2007, which turned out to be great because Miley Cyrus wrote the pop-punk banger "7 Things" about Nick, and that song is a modern karaoke classic. Also, "Lovebug" may or may not be about her.

NICK JONAS AND SELENA GOMEZ

Selena Gomez and Nick Jonas were on-again, off-again between 2008 and 2010, but she will live on in infamy in the boy band's history: she starred as Nick's better half in the music video for one of their biggest singles to date, "Burnin' Up." Their beloved sentry and head of security, Big Rob, is also seen in the video courting Selena. I hope they keep in touch, or at least, added each other on Facebook.

WHAT'S THE LESSON HERE?

As an adult, Nick Jonas somehow wed the dreamiest woman on the planet, Indian actor Priyanka Chopra. Joe Jonas married *Game of Thrones* star Sophie Turner in a spontaneous Las Vegas ceremony after the 2019 Billboard Music Awards, ordained by a fake Elvis and attended by EDM DJ Diplo. They also had a real wedding in France. Clearly, the brothers have done well for themselves. And they are totally doing it now, being married and all. Like, *it*. The deed. Intercourse. Lovemaking. Copulation, coitus, porking, diddling, nailing, knobbing off, making whoopee. Good for them.

NICK *VS.*
JOE *VS.* KEVIN (GIRLS)

IF THERE WAS ever a situation to pick your favorite boy band member, the one you'd french if given the opportunity, it is with the Jonas Brothers. Crushing on more than one sibling borders on incest, and while that flies on *Game of Thrones*, it's not exactly boy band–friendly. So, choose your player.

PLAYER ONE: NICK JONAS

Nick Jonas was every mom's favorite Jonas brother. Back in the day and probably now, who knows, I've never met the guy, Nick was sweet, sensitive, quiet, and wore collared shirts. He was simply always ready to meet the parents. He was the brains of the Jonas Brothers operation and, for a long time, was their principal songwriter. Also, Nick's the richest of the trifecta and regularly participates in charity events, including functions for diabetes, which he was diagnosed with in 2005. It's appropriate that Nick is known for his falsetto, too, because he kinda is a falsetto anthropomorphized: impossible for most people to nail but unequivocally attractive and artistically evocative. I think the Jonas Brothers fans who were most emotionally stable preferred Nick of the bunch, as they should.

PLAYER TWO: JOE JONAS

Those devastating looks. Joe is a hunk and a class clown rolled into one. You can't not love him. In the early days of their career, he was positioned between his brothers to connote leadership as the de facto front man. Joe rarely played guitar live: the six-stringed instrument was reserved for his virtuoso brothers so he may use his free hands to articulate his charisma to anyone watching. He was also the most vivacious, outgoing, and funny one of the bunch, and he made it known. Joe's the heartthrob in a trio of heartthrobs, and if your astrological sign is in the water family, you would absolutely let him ruin your life. Joe attracted Joe Girls, the kind who were ready to sneak boys into their room, violating their home's strict "No Boys Allowed" policy and their mom's "Not until you're older. And even then, it's a maybe" speech. Those were the pop music fans who bought thongs and hid them from their parents. They weren't dangerous, but they wanted a boy who could show them a good time, short of under-the-skirt stuff. In a world of vanilla-scented candles, Joe was their three-wick, limited-edition Yankee Candle in lavender-vanilla. Something extra.

PLAYER THREE: KEVIN JONAS

One word: muttonchops. The women who loved Kevin Jonas are the same who adored Chris Kirkpatrick and Howie Dorough. They thrived on the fact that other ladies didn't seem to get his oomph, and somehow that made their love realer, truer, unlike the others. In reality, Kevin was the most accessible of the bunch regardless

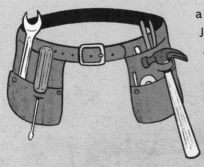

of the fact that he was hitched to a hairdresser from his native New Jersey. (It really could've been *any one* of us!) He was also the romantic of his band, a big brother type, the grounding force, someone who you knew would make a good dad one day the second you saw him. And though picking a fave has nothing to do with heteronormative biology—who wants to bring a kid into the cruel, unsympathetic hellscape that is planet Earth?—Kevin was always a *daddy*. He's definitely warned some kids about "stranger danger" before, and that's enough to make anyone want to drop trou. He also worked as Kathy Wakile's contractor, making an appearance on *The Real Housewives of New Jersey*, which is sexy in a he-definitely-owns-a-tool-belt way.

LET'S BE HONEST, any selection will lead you to victory. Go forth, young warrior.

RIP THE COMPETITION: BIG TIME RUSH, THE WANTED, AND THE BANDS THAT DIDN'T REALLY MAKE IT

After it became clear that the Jonas Brothers claimed seats at both the coveted pop-punk and boy band tables, a bunch of other dudes in impossibly tight cigarette pants wanted in. Finally, they thought, there was a way to rock *and* be beloved by young women everywhere, not only those patrons of Whisky a Go Go. Nice one, brah. Other boy bands of different genres began cropping up, too, simply because it seemed like the world was ready for them again. None of the JoBro-era acts made it as big as the trio, but many became one-hit wonders or landed teen television programs. That's better than nothing.

These are the boy bands worth ruminating over and maybe listening to once if you're feeling sentimental for a time before you had to worry about student loan debt and figure out how taxes work.

BIG TIME RUSH

Like the Monkees, 2Gether, and the Jonas Brothers themselves, Big Time Rush got their start on television. For them, it was Disney's slightly edgier rival, Nickelodeon, where "edgy" is defined by "slime and other gross liquids, poured on its stars' bodies and feet with shocking regularity." Kicking off in 2009 and running for four seasons, *Big Time Rush* followed four hockey-playing BFFs from Minnesota—Kendall Knight, James Diamond, Carlos Garcia, and Logan Mitchell—who were hand-picked by the fictional hot shot Rocque Records producer Gustavo Rocque to move to Los Angeles and become the next big boy band sensation. If this sounds somewhat similar to the plot of *Jonas* to you, well, you're not wrong. *Big Time Rush* had a more "fish out of water" duende, but even its surreal, aspirational script couldn't last forever.

WERE THEY A ONE-HIT WONDER? This may come as a shock, but no. Their debut album, *BTR*, was released by Sony/Columbia and totally blew up with hits like "Worldwide," "Boyfriend," and the self-titled "Big Time Rush." I know. Wild.

MINDLESS BEHAVIOR

The R&B boy band formula experienced its own revival in the early '10s with Mindless Behavior, a quartet-turned-trio of teenagers with more swagger than everyone else on this list combined. Their debut album, 2011's *#1 Girl*, out when members Prodigy, Ray Ray, Princeton, and Roc Royal were just fourteen and fifteen years old, hit number 7 on the Billboard 200. Mindless Behavior's success proved to be only temporary, likely because some of their songs veered on *Kidz Bop* territory…if *Kidz Bop* had some soul. They were fun!

WERE THEY A ONE-HIT WONDER? As much as it pains me to admit to it, yeah. "Mrs. Right," featuring Diggy Simmons, was their only hit to break the Billboard Hot 100.

THE VAMPS

Though English band the Vamps didn't get their start until the Jonas Brothers were on their last leg of existence, there are over-whelming similarities. Both bands play their own instruments. Guitarist James McVey (who once dated Joe's wife Sophie Turner) was already in the music business when he decided he wanted to lead a band instead of simply performing solo, which screams Nick

Jonas. Brotherless, he turned to YouTube and Facebook to find boys to collaborate with, and he did: lead singer Brad Simpson, drummer Tristian Evans, and bassist Connor Bell. His group signed to Mercury/Virgin EMI Records. The Vamps topped the UK charts, but they never became as huge as their team probably envisioned them to become stateside. I'd characterize their sound as PG pop-rock in the early days, PG-13 in the latter half.

WERE THEY A ONE-HIT WONDER? Nope. American fans might only recall their collaborations with Shawn Mendes, "Oh Cecilia (Breaking My Heart)," and Demi Lovato, "Somebody to You," but they've been consistently performing well back home for years.

THE WANTED

UK dance-pop boy band the Wanted was positioned to rival One Direction despite the fact that they predated the "Best Song Ever" band by a year. (They formed in 2009, at the tail end of the Jonas Brothers.) In 2011, the Wanted became a one-hit wonder with the EDM track "Glad You Came," an up-tempo radio hit I don't tire of hearing in European airports. Unfortunately, their legacy is limited to the sexually ambiguous song title (heh, cum) and a party-heavy music video. You could argue that the quintet of Max George, Siva Kaneswaran, Jay McGuiness, Tom Parker, and Ariana Grande's ex-boyfriend Nathan Sykes helped pave new territory for others to traverse: perhaps boy band fans could be open to some hyper-sexual musical style, as long as it is muted in an ejaculation meta-phor and not outright. Or not. They only had one hit, after all.

WERE THEY A ONE-HIT WONDER? In the dictionary definition. Maybe not in the UK, but for the rest of the world, definitely.

CHAPTER SEVEN

LIVE WHILE WE'RE YOUNG: ONE DIRECTION

ONCE, THERE WAS nothing. Then there was something. There was everything. The big bang created the universe. The spectacular explosion, the smallest singularity, inflated for nearly 14 billion years. That time might as well have been filled with darkness, because it wasn't until 2010 that one Irish lad and four young Brits from working-class families—Mullingar, Ireland's Niall Horan, the cute one; Wolverhampton's Liam Payne, the responsible one; Bradford's Zayn Malik, the shy one; Doncaster's Louis Tomlinson, the class clown/bad boy; and Redditch's Harry Styles, the heartthrob—auditioned as soloists on the seventh season of *The X Factor*. Who could have known that the cosmic microwave called existence would zap up a reality singing competition show, leading to the most glorious time in the universe, the creation of One Direction?

Separately, *X Factor* judges Simon Cowell, Cheryl Cole, and Louis Walsh couldn't continue to advance the teenage boys in good faith. They were all talented, but not yet great, and they

ZAYN

obviously couldn't dance. Malik especially. Then, an epiphany: Simon Cowell (or Simon Cowell *and* guest judge/Pussycat Doll Nicole Scherzinger, if you take her account as the truth) had the idea to group Niall, Liam, Zayn, Louis, and Harry together to form a harmonic quintet, the youngest boy band the show had ever seen.

That decision, rumored to have taken Cowell ten minutes to come up with, would prove to be one of the most rewarding, simple experiments in modern pop music history. After two weeks in the show's "boot camp" program after auditions—an accelerated timeline for burgeoning friendships, let alone collaborative careers—something clicked. A cover of Natalie Imbruglia's "Torn" later, and One Direction ("1D" if you're nasty) was official. They came in third place on the show, but that didn't matter.[*] They had something much more gargantuan in store.

Losing the *X Factor* in December 2010 was a pivotal moment for 1D. At the time, there weren't many popular male vocal

---

[*] As Georgina Gregory notes, reality TV singing competitions allow fans to feel like they had some say in the formation of boy bands, that they were there from the very start. In the case of One Direction, fans got to see them learn to dance and sing together, the kind of insider-y rehearsals and early day footage previously unprocurable, let alone witnessed in real time. (Not to mention, they have bragging rights to lord over Directioners who got to the fandom late in the group's career.) Losing has a positive effect, too: who doesn't love to support an underdog? In fact, it's generally unremarked upon in their history, but the Backstreet Boys were rejected from 1993's version of *The X Factor*, *Star Search*. Clearly, there's a history of boy bands going—*and failing*—on these shows.

groups in the UK, save for an embryonic version of the Wanted and JLS. Short for Jack the Lad Swing, the R&B-pop group of adult men couldn't really be deemed a boy band, so the need was there. Cowell, an industry Svengali in his own right, instantly saw One Direction's potential. (Not to knock his know-how, but with hundreds of girls lining up for them outside of the *X Factor* studio during the competition, it would've been hard to miss.) He signed the boy band to his Sony Music record label imprint, Syco Records, in January 2011 in the UK. Turns out, it was great timing for Cowell as well: another Syco boy band, Westlife, recently announced their retirement. He needed a new group just as much as One Direction needed to capitalize on their nascent popularity. A few months later, One Direction was signed to Columbia Records stateside. With the exception of the Jonas Brothers, American audiences really hadn't seen a monolithic boy band since *NSYNC. They needed them, too.

And so, at the beginning of 2011, One Direction got to work. Cowell put them in touch with hit American songwriter Savan Kotecha, a Max Martin protege, who, with a small team, produced their debut single, "What Makes You Beautiful." The song, released on September 11, was exactly what the young group required to not only sustain their hype post–*X Factor* but deliver on it: an affirming, high-energy, no-nonsense, perfect piece of pop that made them appear sweet, sensitive, and attainable, the kind of boys who put women on a pedestal. If there is a better way of encapsulating exactly what a girl needs to hear while coming to terms with the absolute horror show that is heterosexuality during puberty,

HARRY

when the world begins to instruct her to hate herself, I have yet to hear it. The video, too, was playful with modest touches of sensuality (it doesn't hurt that it was filmed on the same stretch of beach as Blink-182's parodic "All the Small Things," an Easter egg for boy band fans if there ever was one). Kotecha told *Billboard* that the secret to "What Makes You Beautiful" and boy band music in general is doing "the exact opposite of what's going on… teenage girls need to feel it's their own thing." Radio was dominated by Rihanna, Adele, and LMFAO's "Party Rock Anthem," so he certainly accomplished that.

A combination of marketing, momentum, and music so joyful it should come with a warning for serotonin secretions, One Direction released their debut LP, *Up All Night*, with "What Makes You Beautiful" and the lovelorn, rock-tinged "One Thing." The album shot up the charts in the UK in 2011 and in 2012, debuted at number 1 in the US, making them the first English group to ever debut atop the charts with their first album. Really think about that for a moment. The Beatles never even did this shit.

When One Direction voyaged to North America later that year, they inspired their own sort of Beatlemania. Actually, it might've been even grander because of the advent of social media and their brilliant utilization of it. One Direction's unedited Justin Bieber–esque Twitter sharing led fans to believe they were close to the boys, an illusion of access more palpable than even what watching their *X Factor* auditions provided. Fans felt more like friends, a priceless connection in the boy band universe. As a result, every arena tour One Direction booked sold out in a

LIAM

NIALL

split second. Women would camp outside their hotels waiting for a glimpse of the group, fully enamored with the chaotic boy band that couldn't even dance. There was no stopping them because their meteoric rise was completely unprecedented and unchallenged, minus a minor trademark infringement lawsuit from an American band also called One Direction. They settled, those nerds disappeared, and in May 2012, One Direction began recording their second album, setting the pace for what would become their normal: an exhaustive, accelerated album-tour-album-tour schedule that might even impress the boy bands who laid the framework a decade prior. *Take Me Home* was released in November. It, too, debuted at number 1 on the Billboard 200.

One Direction fever was unstoppable. "Live While We're Young" was a brilliant follow-up smash single to "What Makes You Beautiful." Lyrically, it was a brief detour from telling a girl she's great to having a wonderful time with her, free of the responsibilities of adulthood. Here, the One Direction boys' personalities really began to shine through. They were a bit anarchic. You could really get into trouble with them, with no bigger consequences than lunch detention. They even tamed the ever elusive rock ballad in "Little Things," which, in November 2012, they sang for the queen of England.

A year, a 3-D concert documentary so huge it was released in theaters, and a few massive arena tours later, One Direction released their third LP, *Midnight Memories*, in November 2013. Once again, as you most certainly guessed, it debuted at number 1, making One Direction the first group in history to debut atop the charts with their first three records. At this stage, 1D had graduated to stadiums, with tens of thousands of seats. A remarkable feat off the support of a few unrivaled singles, including their best-known track, the appropriately named "Best Song Ever." (It really was the best song ever.)

In 2014, keeping with their strategy, the band released their fourth album and once again, it debuted at number 1. The release, *Four*, is most noteworthy for the fan frenzy that turned the up-tempo, Louis Tomlinson–led song "No Control" into a single when it wasn't originally marketed to be one. (I'm no tinhatter, but perhaps it had something to do with the song's lyric of "Waking up / Beside you I'm a loaded gun," which is less like the Boyzone song "Loaded Gun" and definitely a metaphor for…One Erection.) Directioners demanded the track get a full release, and it did. That's paramount, and so is this: if you're into numerology-based fore-shadowing, the album title suggested the heartbreak that was yet to come. In March 2015, after months of embarking on one of the largest, most successful tours of all time, attended by 3.4 million ticket buyers, a hubristic Zayn Malik announced he was leaving the group because he wanted to be "a normal 22-year-old who is able to relax and have some private time out of the spotlight," or so it was written in his official statement. Now there were only four.

Saddened by the loss of their bandmate and, well, best mate, Louis, Liam, Harry, and Niall went back into the studio and released One Direction's fifth and final album in 2015, without Zayn. *Made in the A.M.* (After Malik?) is a hybrid folk-rock-pop self-homage to the group's legacy and a gorgeous farewell to the fans responsible for their fame. The video for the single "History" made it clear that this was the end. Imagine an intimate slideshow, a collection of images of the boy band throughout their career, beginning with their *X Factor* auditions, and ending with the image of them hugging, the final four members walking away in separate directions and amicably waving goodbye to one another. Lyrically, "History" doubles as a grateful breakup anthem (clever boys, these) and possesses a chorus that reminds me of Randy Newman's *Toy Story* tune, "You've Got a Friend in Me." For 1D fans, thinking about it is enough to evoke tears. Not that I'm speaking from personal experience or anything.

One Direction announced they'd embark on a hiatus beginning in March 2016, exactly one year after Zayn left the group. In the time since, each boy has tried his hand at the solo music thing with varying degrees of success: Zayn pursued the R&B-affected pop that he always loved and 1D never attempted; Harry went full Bowie, desiring vintage rock-and-roll mystique that, as the most public face of 1D, he was never granted; Louis and Niall stuck to pop-rock; and Liam flirted with EDM and hip-hop. Styles is the closest to anything like a Timberlake, but they're much too different to really compare. The similarities start and stop at their like-minded star power and how, after leaving a boy band, they were able to transgress a fickle pop music space and become critically acclaimed without abandoning the fans that brought them to the top.

In their five short years as a band, One Direction became one of the biggest boy bands the world had ever seen, a big bang in their own right. But would anyone be able to do it like them again?

LOUIS

Conspiracy Corner: March 25, Larry Stylinson, and the Internet

THERE IS NO shortage of conspiracy theories in the One Direction camp, up to and including your run-of-the-mill Illuminati accusations. Choosing to engage with these, however, is nothing more than the practice everyone participates in when they read a gossip headline and question the validity of it while purchasing an $8 bottle of red wine and two frozen stuffed-crust pizzas at the grocery store on a Friday night. Directioners *might* take it a few steps further. They *might* choose to make and argue for connections where there *might* not be any, ignoring contrary evidence, all in an effort to corroborate beliefs they hold dear. It should go without saying that these theories should be taken in jest and can absolutely be harmful to those involved, in a *basement full of newspaper clippings and Post-it notes connected by red string* kind of way.

March 25

Dim your lamps and light a candle. If there ever was a more cursed date on the calendar, a Directioner has yet to hear it. On March 25, 2015, Zayn Malik announced his departure from One Direction. Exactly one year later, the band would embark on their own indefinite hiatus, a two-word phrase so frightening that Directioners would rather you never utter it, like the wizarding world would rather you never speak Voldemort's name. The message was clear, and they broke up. On the same date in 2016, Zayn Malik dropped *Mind of Mine*, his debut solo LP. On March 25, 2017, a teaser for Harry Styles's debut solo single, "Sign of the Times," hit the internet. That same day, Liam Payne revealed he was a father. Coincidence, conspiracy, or erudite marketing? Potentially all of the above?

Larry Stylinson

Of all the conspiracy theories One Direction has brought upon the internet, none is quite as omnipresent as the belief that Harry Styles and Louis Tomlinson are in a relationship and have been since the beginning of the group. The theory is so popular that one of the most retweeted tweets of all time is simply Louis wishing Harry well with "Always in my heart @Harry_Styles. Yours sincerely, Louis," sent in October 2011. Larries, or Larry Stylinson shippers, believe the message is indisputable proof that the two were and are together, despite the fact that neither party has vocalized an interest in men and have only ever publicly part- nered with women. When Tomlinson began dating Eleanor Calder in September 2011, one year into the band's existence, Larries believed she was acting as a beard, though Louis assured fans that he wasn't hiding homosexuality. He likes women.

In the band's earliest days, Louis and Harry could be seen physically near one another, placed shoulder to shoulder in portraits, playfully touching elbows and gazing upon each other's perfectly sculpted mugs. Within a few years, the pair were photo- graphed far from each other, in a move Larries presume was calculated by their management company, Modest, in an attempt to bury their romance and control their outward appearance. Larries suspect homophobia is to blame and say that by silencing their relationship, Modest effectively sent the message that queerness is wrong. Larries also believe there's something to be said about Harry and Louis's similar tattoos, which they suspect substantiates their relationship: Harry's birdcage and Louis's birds, Harry's anchor and Louis's rope, Harry's ship and Louis's compass, so on and so forth. I think it's irrefutable proof of a nautical, Americana theme and interest in rockabilly iconography, ink you can acquire at any tattoo parlor anywhere.

Even though the band is no longer active, Larries persist, dedicated to their beliefs. In 2015, when Tomlinson revealed that he was expecting his first child with girlfriend Briana Jungwirth, fans speculated that she was faking a pregnancy. When obscured photographs of the child emerged, some theorized that it was a doll and dubbed the movement "Babygate." Years later, Freddie Reign Tomlinson is very much real and alive, but the belief that Louis and Harry will one day be free to express their love for one another remains.

BEST DATE EVER: ONE DIRECTION AND THE ROMANCES THAT KILLED US

Unlike most boy bands past and present, One Direction spent much of their time in the limelight wifed up with babes who, when they weren't receiving death threats from obsessive fans, were a constant source of tabloid fodder. I don't envy these women's experiences, but then I remember they were smooching a 1D boy for a few years (or in the case of Harry, a few months), and think it's worth weighing the pros and cons. They had to make sacrifices to date young English royalty, and just being a woman online, with or without Louis making you a cuppa in the other room, is enough to inspire venom and vitriol. Regardless, it's high time the girlfriends of yore get the respect they deserve for making it out alive, because the hate they received was unjust. These women should've never been demonized. Also: Haylor forever.

LOUIS TOMLINSON AND ELEANOR CALDER (2012–2015, 2017–?)

Eleanor Calder wasn't famous when she met the cheeky Louis Tomlinson, but by the time of their split, she was the source material for endless fan sites and something of a social media celebrity-turned-model. Legend has it Harry Styles played match-maker and got them together through mutual friends. Louis and Eleanor broke up because of the geographic distance between them (remember, they dated smack dab in the midst of 1D's endless touring schedule), but they rekindled things post–One

Direction, in 2017, a particular kind of love story that doesn't get enough shine. It speaks volumes, too, that they got back together around the time of Louis's mother's and sister's untimely passing.

LOUIS TOMLINSON AND BRIANA JUNGWIRTH (2015)

Louis and Briana, a hairstylist, dated very briefly in 2015 when she became pregnant, and Louis became a father...*But did he become a father?*

He did. #Babygate was a fun conspiracy theory, but he's definitely a dad. Freddie was born in January 2016.

LOUIS TOMLINSON AND DANIELLE CAMPBELL (2015-2017)

Louis and Danielle, an actor on the CW series *The Originals*, dated for nearly two years. Their relationship was unremarkable at best, but it did confirm what Louis stans have always known to be true: he's a serial monogamist, or he's always in a relationship to cover up the fact that he and Harry Styles are in love, depending on your cabal.

LIAM PAYNE AND DANIELLE PEAZER (2010-2012)

Liam and Danielle met while auditioning on *The X Factor*, and who doesn't love a reality TV show romance? They called it quits after a tumultuous, on-and-off-again relationship. She became a health and fitness YouTube influencer a few years after their breakup, which is exactly how she should spend her time.

LIAM PAYNE AND SOPHIA SMITH (2013-2015)

Yet another fairy-tale relationship, as far as teen dreaming is concerned: Sophiam, better known as Liam Payne and Sophia

Smith. They knew each other in grade school and got together for a whirlwind romance in the midst of Payne's mega fame. Like Louis and Eleanor before them, Sophiam had to call it quits because of the distance. She should absolutely write a YA novel about it and turn it into a screenplay.

LIAM PAYNE AND CHERYL COLE (2016–2018)

Yes, Liam dated one of the *X Factor* judges who helped create One Direction and whom he first met at age fourteen. Payne has always had an affinity for older women (at one point he was linked to super-model Naomi Campbell, but that was never confirmed, despite how much joy it would bring me) and the Chiam age gap definitely nourished red tops, or UK tabloids, for a while. Together, Chiam had a child, Liam's first, on March 22, 2017. His name is Bear Grey Payne.

HARRY STYLES AND TAYLOR SWIFT (2012–2013)

For a few glorious months in late 2012 until January 2013, the juiciest of all 1D relationships past and present overwhelmed Directioners every-where. Haylor, the partnering of Harry Styles and Taylor Swift, was born. Prior to Swift, Styles had his fair share of short-lived flings (there was his first girlfriend, Abigail

Crawshaw, in 2007; Felicity Skinner in 2010; television host Caroline Flack in 2011; Wilhelmina model Emma Ostilly in 2012, and so on), but nothing hit the fandom as hard as the T-Swift and H-Styles meeting of minds. They broke up, obviously, and she's purportedly written a lot of music about their romantic affair. Swift's song "Style" is a treasure trove of relationship allusions over an alluring major-chord chorus.

Addendum: Four years after their split, Swift recorded a sexy duet with Zayn Malik for the *Fifty Shades of Grey* soundtrack, "I Don't Wanna Live Forever," a real full-circle moment. Since then, Styles has been linked to his fair share of models, including Kendall Jenner, but Haylor was and still is the only relationship worth mourning.

NIALL HORAN AND ELLIE GOULDING (2013)

Niall and Ellie were a match made in English pop heaven. The pair only went on a few dates but it was enough to crush the hearts of girls everywhere who adored young Horan. Especially American girls, with whom he was outrageously popular.

NIALL HORAN AND SELENA GOMEZ (2016...MAYBE?)

This one is also tricky, and Niall is a pro at keeping his affairs under wraps. Or is it that his boy band brethren are really bad at it? Allegedly, if the gossip rags are to be believed, Niall and Selena were an item. They're good friends now, as are Ellie and Niall. Maybe Horan is simply the best ex-boyfriend a girl could ask for.

ZAYN MALIK AND PERRIE EDWARDS (2011–2015)

Zayn and Perrie met at the *X Factor* season 8 finale, when her girl group Little Mix was about to take home the big prize and One Direction was invited back to the stage for a performance. In the years that followed, Zayn and Perrie really acted like they had found their person. He got her face tattooed on his body. They got engaged in 2013. The pair ended up breaking things off in 2015, the same year Zayn left One Direction. Perrie claimed he broke up with her over text message (way to one-up Joe Jonas on the cowardice scale!), but he denied it. He also covered up the tattoo, so, uh, nothing to see here.

ZAYN MALIK AND GIGI HADID (2015–2018)

Not long after his split with Perrie, Zayn began dating supermodel Gigi Hadid, which proved to really work in his favor. She starred in the music video for his debut solo single, "Pillowtalk," and the pair were inseparable on red carpets, even rocking corresponding high-fashion robot costumes at the 2016 Met Gala. But like One Direction before them, all good things come to an end, and they broke things off, affably, after three years. They've been seen together since, but there's no proof she's his Eleanor. Not yet, anyway.

Style Watch

ONE DIRECTION'S FASHION evolution is a sight to behold, and all five of them deserve medals of bravery for making it out alive. They were styled more like the Spice Girls than any other pop group: each boy was given a totally different outfit to highlight his persona, which means there are a myriad of looks to pull from and no real homogeneity. In the end days of 1D, Harry Styles no doubt rose to the top of the group as its most stylish member. And for that reason, here's his look from the 2014 American Music Awards.

* From the very beginning of the band, Harry wore preppy blazers and bow ties. As time went on, he adopted a much more rock-and-roll take on the coming-home-to-mama style, and thank goodness he did. May he never lose his esteem for a structured jacket with cool, feminine detailing, amen.

* I'm thrilled to report that with One Direction, boy bands finally figured out how to wear pants. Gone are the days where you could hide a fan in one of your trousers' legs, and gone are the days of having to put your pants on while lying down because they are so unbearably tight. There's freedom in a smart fit.

* Most of One Direction started rocking ankle-height, pointed-toe Chelsea boots in the later portion of their career, but Styles really treasured them. He's known for his Yves Saint Laurent footwear worth more than my life and yours combined, and nothing screams gratuitous wealth like sparkly, glittery kicks. Display them in the Metropolitan Museum of Art so I may visit infrequently and shed a single tear in their glow.

MICK JAGGER-INSPIRED STRUCTURED JACKET
IMPECCABLY TAILORED TROUSERS
HARRY STYLES
YSL BOOTIES THAT SHINE BRIGHTER THAN THE SUN

QUEER DIRECTION

Queer fans experience their own marginalization within the already maligned tribe of the boy band obsessed, even though loving a boy band isn't limited to sexual interest and that boy band appreciation is meant to be an escape from the hegemonic masculinity and other baloney that pervades popular music. In the same way that queer boy band members have historically waited until after the band was finished to come out for fear of alienating fans, queer boy band fans can feel isolated expressing their fandom. There is no perfect solution, no exemplar boy band. When One Direction came around, however, it was easy to feel like they were pretty close. And that's because of their fans.

Fan fiction is an inevitability in the internet era* and has proven to be a positive, community-building force for queer fans. Observing, fantasizing, and writing about the loving looks of Larry Stylinson; imagining them to be a real relationship; or entertaining the possibility that boy band members themselves might be closeted reflects the experience of many queer youths coming into their own sexual identity. ("Are they keeping a secret like me?") These exercises allow queer fans to experience representation on a mainstream scale, likely for the first time. It's no wonder, then, that

---

* In the case of one twenty-something Harry Styles superfan turned published author, Anna Todd, fan fiction became grounds for a real-life *New York Times* best-seller and movie deal. Her fanfic, *After*, in which a sheltered college freshman falls for a motorcycle jacket–clad ruffian named Harry—Hardin Scott in the novelization—became a huge hit on Wattpad. The site claims *After* has been read over 1.5 billion times. I tried to read it one time and couldn't get past the grammatical errors. The movie, on the other hand, was good and horny, and I genuinely recommend seeing it.

One Direction became a popular act for drag kings to parody. If you're ever in the Bay Area, the group Every Direction is worth your time, attention, and money.

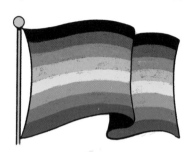

Of course, queer fandom doesn't only live online or at bars in progressive cities. In the case of One Direction, it mobilized quickly. As Brodie Lancaster chronologized for MTV, a Directioner named Li launched Rainbow Direction in 2013, an organization run by a "diverse group of fans committed to equality and inclusiveness." They sought to make "[the One Direction] fandom a safe and enjoyable place for LGBTQ+ fans with education, action and visibility." Over the course of 1D's tenure, Li and their fellow Rainbow Directioners organized over two hundred meet-ups across One Direction's 2014 and 2015 worldwide tours, bringing together nearly eight thousand fans dedicated to discussing inclusivity, showing visibility, and providing resources for questioning youth. Their impact was so great, Lancaster notes, that those fans have gone on to run campaigns on tours for Taylor Swift, Troye Sivan, Ed Sheeran, Little Mix, and solo 1D members. It's likely that if you've patronized a teen pop stadium or arena show since 2013, you've seen a barrage of rainbow flags, clothing, face paint, and glitter on attendees. It's reflective of a change in culture and the lasting legacy of One Direction's queer fans.

THEY LOOK SO PERFECT: 5 SECONDS OF SUMMER

Where there are teenage boys, there are guitars. And where there are cute teenage boys with asymmetrical haircuts masking the majority of their cute faces because they cannot bear the weight of the world—everything is the worst, Mom and Dad just don't understand, ugh, can't wait to get out of this town—there are sappy pop-punk songs about unrequited love and suburban mundanity to learn on those guitars. Enter 5 Seconds of Summer, whose group name alone should send the shiver of an early '00s emo flashback down your spine. (To save all of us some time, the shorthand for the group's unnecessarily long name is 5SOS, pronounced "five-sauce" and not "five-S-O-S." There is no method to this madness. Just boy things.) The Australian band formed in 2011, when rhythm guitarist Luke Hemmings, bassist Calum Hood, and lead guitarist Michael Clifford met in grade school at Norwest Christian College outside of Sydney. The trio started jamming and filming song covers to post on YouTube, tracks that included Wheatus's "Teenage Dirtbag," work by Mike Posner and the dreadful Chris Brown. Later that year, they were joined by a mutual friend, the slightly older drummer Ashton Irwin, whom they so desperately needed in order to play live. A band was made.

5 Seconds of Summer appeared to be as self-starting as a budding boy band could be. Based on good looks and great hooks alone, they managed to grow to forty thousand Facebook followers in a matter of months. They gigged locally. By June 2012, they released a debut EP, the acoustic *Unplugged*, including the two original tracks "Gotta Get Out" and "Too Late," as well as covers of Blink-182's "I Miss You" and the pop-punk boy band All Time Low's "Jasey Rae." They released a second EP, *Somewhere New,* with a few more new tracks, including the early single "Out of My Limit." A few tweets from One Direction members in support of the project later, and in 2013, it was revealed that the home-grown band of boys from down under would open for 1D on their Take Me Home arena world tour. That same year, 5SOS signed to major label Capitol Records and got to work on a debut LP. Around Valentine's Day in 2014, they released their debut single as a signed band, "She Looks So Perfect," just in time for Directioners to fall in love with them. They joined One Direction on yet another worldwide tour. That summer, it was stadiums.

"She Look So Perfect" was 5SOS's "What Makes You Beautiful." The song became their easily traceable, career-making moment, but it's also much weirder than the 1D banger. The song is by-the-book pop-punk, including a bombastic, sing-along chorus and lyrics that reference things the band is far too young to have experienced. (The best line: "I made a mixtape straight out of '94 / I got your ripped skinny jeans lying on my floor.") It is not punk in the traditional sense, *like, at all,* and it is so overwhelmingly pop that one riff is grounds for addiction. When their self-titled debut album dropped in June 2014, the teen girls who loved 1D had already made space for 5SOS in their hearts, iTunes libraries, and Spotify playlists.

From there, the ascent was swift. They adopted One Direction's schedule: an album and worldwide stadium tour each year, lather, rinse, repeat. That changed when One Direction called it quits in 2016, and 5 Seconds of Summer decided the go-go-go style of their parent boy band was not for them. Instead of continuing to push the limits of their girl-positive, mom-friendly pop-punk, 5SOS took a break. They emerged on the cover of *Rolling Stone* with a profile that made them out to be Menudo in the streets and Mötley Crüe in the sheets in an era when rock-and-roll hedonism could not be more passé, and rebranded themselves as an EDM-but-also-sometimes-Industrial-leaning pop-rock group. The boy band title stuck, but only for a while, and those fans who found themselves more in the 5SOS camp than team 1D remained loyal to them even as they navigated an unfamiliar, mature musical identity.

The band's new look suggested another form of retirement for boy bands: you don't need to disappear for years. You could leave while you're at the top and return anew, even if the thing you come back to doesn't hit those teen girl checkmarks as directly as, say, a song about a perfect-looking partner and American Apparel underwear. You can change.

AND THAT'S WHAT MAKES YOU(R) BOY BAND ECONOMY

Though the groups have always been sonically and aesthetically different, there was absolutely no denying that by 2014 One Direction's audience had fully embraced the mall punk edge of 5 Seconds of Summer to become fans of their group, too, not unlike the rare Backstreet Boys fan who found room in their CD collection for some *NSYNC. But the Backstreet Boys never brought *NSYNC out on stadium tours. They were positioned as rivals, whereas Cowell and the 1D boys played it smart. They supported the 5SOS brand, because they wanted to invest in it, buy into it, and reap the financial benefits. Think of it as a double payday that doesn't cost much more than a few tour dates and supportive tweets every once in a while. Someone's gotta open for you, so why not cash in on them? Now, name all the artists you already support online, *for free*. If you were a better businessperson, your beloved groups would cut you a check.

In 2014, *Billboard* reported that all five members of One Direction owned a share of London-based company 5SOS LLC, a whopping 50 percent of its 120 shares. The other 50 percent is held by Modest Management, the same UK company that represents both 1D and 5SOS. Since then, fans and music business folk alike have questioned the accuracy of the financial break-down, but whatever the case, 1D owns part of 5SOS. Regarding 5 Seconds of Summer's origins, that really makes sense: they were already signed to a major label and raking in plentiful pay with their first EP, and they were assisted by a Louis Tomlinson tweet in November 2012 that linked to "Gotta Get Out." (Niall Horan gave them the cosign on their second EP days later.) Without the 1D endorsement, who knows if they would've enjoyed the success they've had. I'd like to say it's great that boy bands have found a way to play nice and bolster each other, but if the good deed wasn't chained to their wallets, would they ever? Do they even like each other? (They do.) Am I trying to launch a new conspiracy theory? (I am not.) Is this even worth interrogating? (Probably not.) There's truly no business like show business in late capitalism.

CHAPTER EIGHT

MIC DROP: BTS AND THE K-POP EXPLOSION

THE RISE OF K-POP

UP UNTIL THE mid-2010s, English-language groups dominated global understanding of boy bands. Western countries have ruled the international pop music market as long as there has been one for young people to participate in, and boy band history has very distinct American and British roots. That doesn't mean that Korean pop music is a new fascination, by any stretch, just that it has only recently become popularized for audiences that haven't looked beyond the Atlantic Ocean for swoon-worthy sounds. Some Korean pop stars actually date back to the 1950s, such as a vocal group called the Kim Sisters, whose English-language covers scored them over twenty visits to *The Ed Sullivan Show* in the 1960s, nearly as many visits as Jim Henson's Muppets. They were Kermit-big. (Unfortunately, the Kim Sisters' popularity bordered on orientalism; they wore Chinese cheongsam and performed African American spirituals for US troops.) What you're likely most familiar with, and what this section tackles, is contemporary K-pop, which dates back to 1992, a year before the Backstreet Boys were a twinkle in Lou Pearlman's eye. That's also twenty years before Psy's parodic "Gangnam Style" became a household hit and a viral horse-riding dance move.

Unlike a broad history of boy bands, K-pop's origins are most often traced back to a single date and performance: April 11, 1992, the day the group Seo Taiji and Boys debuted on a televised talent show for the Munhwa Broadcasting Corporation (MBC), one of South Korea's three television networks at the time and one of the very few ways the Korean public could interact with popular culture. Before Taiji and his boys blew minds across the country with their rap song "Nan Arayo" (in English, "I Know"), Korean pop dared not to be expressive or face extreme consequences. Music in the '80s was controlled by dictator Chun Doo-hwan, who acquired power in a military coup in 1979 and ruled until 1988, when South Korea became a democracy. Chun allowed only "healthy songs" with positive political and nationalistic messages, or innocent songs with no room for sexual posturing done in the traditional musical style called trot, *ppongjjak*, to air publicly. (Prior to Chun's rule, another dictator, President Park Chung-hee, who ruled from 1962 through 1979, banned all rock music because he viewed the genre as a form of protest. You can only imagine how creatively stifling that must've been, and why Herculean pop was able to take over so rapidly.) Seo Taiji and Boys planted the seed that would eventually become the towering, revolutionary K-pop industry by marrying old-school hip-hop, pop, break dancing, performing as a group instead of as a solo act, and implementing their own original work on MBC for

all their country to see. And to think, the judges on the show gave them the lowest score possible.

"Nan Arayo" became a hit, anyway, and so did Seo Taiji and Boys. They were lovingly named the Korean New Kids on the Block in the press, and as they grew in popularity, so did their confidence. Their 1995 hit "Come Back Home" introduced gangster rap to South Korea. Lyrically, the single attacked social ills without placating ("My rage toward this society / Is getting greater and greater / Finally, it turned into disgust / Truths disappear at the tip of the tongue"), a move that would've been incomprehensible three years prior. In 1996, they called it quits (in true boy band fashion they only existed for five years), but their legacy was already cemented.

In 1995, South Korean record producer Soo-man Lee (known as Chairman Lee within his organization, which speaks to the authority of company heads in a more direct way than I ever could) founded SM Entertainment with the idea that music could continue to help South Korea thrive if it were sold to the world as a cultural commodity. His first project was a boy band called H.O.T. (short for High-Five of Teenagers), who became the first pop group to sell 1 million albums in the country. They largely kicked off the trend of K-pop groups naming themselves with intialisms, à la LFO. This way, Lee's acts would not require translation in other countries, therefore promoting future ubiquity (that really helped one of his biggest boy bands to date, EXO, decades later). In 1996, Seo Taiji and Boys' Yang "Goon" Hyun-suk would follow Chun's suit, forming his own agency, YG Entertainment. In 1997, musician Park Jin-young, known as J. Y. Park, founded JYP Entertainment, and eventually a big three was formed.* Think of these agencies like major labels stateside, just with ultimate creative control and financial assistance from their government in the same way the US bolsters farming and the automotive industry. In 1999, following a financial crisis in which the government took out massive loans from the IMF and owed them big, South Korea passed the Basic Law for the Promotion of Cultural Industries. The policy meant at least 1 percent of the entire state budget would go to the arts, with the understanding that it could be commodified and bring

---

★ For many years there was a big four, including another entertainment agency called DSP Media, founded in 1991. For the sake of clarity, and to focus on music of the mid-to-late 2010s later on in the chapter, I'm choosing to focus on the big three of that era: SM, YG, and JYP.

more money into the country. It was a triumph, and the teen music magazine section of your local chain bookstore is proof.

With that support, K-pop entertainment agencies created a framework for how boy bands and girl groups, or "idol groups," are created. The extremely manufactured process is crucial to the formation of these groups. First, a company scouts potential idols through open casting calls, as they would in an American or English boy band. There's an extensive auditioning process, followed by training—singing, dancing, acting, media training, etiquette courses, and so on—and assembly: taking the top trainees who make it through the wringer and placing them into a group dynamic that will best work for an individual project. Consider it a Korean version of Berry Gordy's Motown mixed with Menudo's mechanization, except that accepted trainees are completely supported by the record company. (That's more Pearlman, without the dishonesty.) Artist contracts, as a result, are usually concrete and completely inflexible, and they span years, sometimes over a decade. In the extreme cases where agreements are ironclad and veer into abusive territory, they're referred to indelicately as "slave contracts." Idol groups work insanely long hours, usually live together, eat together, rehearse together, wake up together, and do the same thing the next day together. The uniformity helps boy bands move like a unit. And if that's not damning enough, perhaps this factoid is: only one in ten trainees makes it to a debut.

Unlike the Western boy bands that sometimes recoil at the designation of "cute one," "shy one," "heartthrob," and "bad boy," K-pop boy band boys accept the titles they're given. And they're much more tangible: there's a leader/face of the group, main/lead/sub vocalists (they all sing, but the main vocalists are the boys with the best pipes, who typically have a wider range and sing most of a song's vocal lines; lead vocalists support them and usually lead the chorus; sub vocalists are beneath them), a dancer (there are no One Directions in K-pop. They all dance, and those designated "the dancer" have the best moves), a rapper (you see where this is going, right?), a *maknae* (the youngest one in the group), so on and so forth. There are also markedly more members than in the West: five boys in the band is almost a minimum requirement in K-pop. Seven to thirteen is a sweet spot. Twenty-five is the age I turned when I gave up trying to memorize all of their names.

As for the sonic composition, each release or era of a K-pop boy band project is high-concept, and every aspect of the group is dedicated to said concept. The expert manufacturing goes even further: K-pop groups re-record songs and reshoot videos, which are necessary for viral fame, in different languages to sell it to different countries. For example, Japanese versions are crucial because the island nation is the second largest music market after the United States. K-pop international hits have English lyrics, too, mostly in the chorus, to hook those audiences. Accessibility to international markets is integral to the K-pop mission.

Musically, K-pop doesn't play it safe: there's hip-hop influence, Swedish pop melodies, EDM, techno, Western and Eastern pop, R&B for ballads, and more…a maximalist, layered approach to pop that puts the hushed, whisper-chanteuses of the 2010s to shame (here's looking at you, Lana Del Rey). As songwriter Rodnae "Chikk" Bell told *Rolling Stone* in 2018, "Korean pop music likes differentiation and changes. The average American song is four melodies, maybe five. The average K-pop song is eight to 10. They are also very heavy in the harmonies." Even K-pop ballads are overproduced, glamorous, seismic. More is always bigger, almost always better, and invariably entertaining.

But it took years for mainstream music markets stateside to fully embrace K-pop superstardom, and it's still a relatively new welcome. Just like how Backstreet Boys broke the '90s boy band mania that defined a specific time in popular music, K-pop hadn't produced a boy band to do the same, though the music had already gone through many eras. That is not to undersell solo artists like Psy, or Rain before him, who is chiefly credited as the first K-pop star to break internationally in the early 2000s, or women like BoA, who sang in English, or girl groups like Girls' Generation, 2NE1, or the Wonder Girls, who first cracked the Billboard Hot 100 in 2009. K-pop was already here. There simply needed to be a boy band to bring the music to new heights, because boy bands are essential to pop music success.

There were some, like Super Junior, TVXQ!, BEAST, 2PM, Big Bang. And then came BTS.

BOYS IN LUV: BTS

Ask any room—for this exercise, preferably a focus group compiled of random Americans—to name a K-pop boy band, and they might utter only one: BTS.

In 2005, after working for Park Jin-young's JYP Entertainment as a composer and producer for nearly a decade, Bang Si-hyuk, aka Hitman Bang, left his job to form his own company: Big Hit Entertainment. Bang experienced a few minor successes in his first few years, and

RM

SUGA

in 2010, decided he wanted to create a boy band that pushed the existing K-pop formula. He wanted to curate a group of "bulletproof Boy Scouts" (in Korean, Bangtan Sonyeondan), an idol group who could not only sing, dance, and act, like all idol groups, but a brave band immune to the criticisms young people face on daily basis. The narrative centered on the idea that the pressure of adolescence rains down like ammo in a war zone (melodramatic!), and this courageously cool group would empower youth to approach life without fear. Not a bad message, but a curiously violent one that feels truer to My Chemical Romance or Green Day's *American Idiot* era than New Edition or *NSYNC.

Over the course of three years, Bang scouted and auditioned trainees for his group of Bangtan Boys, now referred to as Behind the Scene, or BTS. The enterprise began as a rap crew called DaeNamHyup with leader RM, then known as underground rapper Runch Randa, and another MC named Hun-cheal, who went by the stage name Iron. Bang decided to grow the act into a seven-piece boy band and, in 2013, after several members came and went, he completed the group. The roster was final: leader/rapper RM (given name Kim Nam-joon), who at that point had been training for the project for three years; rapper/producer Suga (Min Yoon-gi); rapper/dancer J-Hope (Jung Ho-seok); the *hyung* ("older brother") and *visual* ("heartthrob") Jin (Kim Seok-jin, also known as "worldwide handsome"); vocalist V (Kim Tae-hyung); *maknae* Jungkook (Jeon Jeong-guk); and dancer/vocalist Jimin (Park Ji-min). The septet moved into a dorm together. At the very beginning, they slept in the same room, a living situation that has been normalized in the industry, but still feels like a punishment to me. Things were intense.

On June 9, 2013, BTS's lineup was officially revealed to the public, and on June 11, their debut single, the straight-up gangster rap "No More Dream," and its rough-and-tumble delinquent schoolyard music video were released. The next day, June 12, BTS dropped their debut single album *2 Cool 4 Skool*, the first in their "school trilogy." The release was meant to resonate with kids overwhelmed by societal expectations of them, a move underrepresented in the glossy macrocosm of K-pop, but similar to the critical debauchery Seo Taiji and Boys laid forth twenty years earlier. What speaks to kids more directly than declarations in "the world doesn't understand, everything is fucked, everybody sucks" family? And why did they look so good doing it?

The record had some moderate success, but BTS was an underdog act. (Impossible to believe now, I know, but bear with me. They were a beautiful leafy green sprout not yet sprung from nutritional compost manure; they needed to get through some shit, first.) The K-pop press found their Western hip-hop style and swagger too far removed from their own realities and needlessly aggressive, but it did well enough to inspire the release of their first EP and second installment in the school trilogy, *O!RUL8,2?*, on September 11, 2013, and a second EP and final installment, *Skool Luv Affair*, on February 12, 2014. If dropping that many new releases in a matter of months seems unusual to you, compare it to an American rapper dropping mixtapes between albums. A steady stream of new material, annual US tours at a time when other K-pop acts weren't

J HOPE

doing the same, partnered with a
growing profile and a few reality shows
(*Rookie King: Channel Bangtan* on
South Korean music television channel
SBS MTV in 2013 and *American Hustle
Life* on Mnet and *BTS GO!* on Mnet USA in
2014) made BTS, a new group signed with a
non-big-three entertainment corporation, increasingly unavoidable.

In the summer of 2014, having expended the extent of their
bad schoolboy hijinks, BTS dropped their debut LP, *Dark & Wild*,
ushering in a new era for the group: a softer approach to their
hard-core hip-hop roots and a gesture that more pop sensibilities
were brewing. (Mind you: their newfound soft edge wasn't totally
the result of label pressure. BTS and Bang have long prided themselves on being a transgressive boy band with some freedoms,
like posting on their own social media accounts, especially the
dialog-building Twitter, when other acts have management do
the street team work. It also doesn't hurt that they're beautiful
boys who appear gentle, even while performing truculent tunes.
A sonic balance simply made more sense for them.) Their foray
into hip-hop pop arrived in 2015 in the form of two EPs, *The
Most Beautiful Moment in Life, Part 1* and *Part 2*,
released in April and November, respectively.
In December, *Pt. 2* hit number 171 on the
Billboard 200 chart, something no K-pop
band outside of the big-three entertainment agencies had done before.

BTS, with the help of their loyal
fandom, called the ARMY (Adorable
Representative M.C. for Youth) were

JUNGKOOK

bolstering themselves to major label heights. By the end of 2015, BTS was huge on social media and only getting bigger. Mainstream fame was fast approaching. It arrived in 2016 with their second studio album, *Wings*. Once again, BTS broke a Billboard 200 record: it debuted at number 26 on the chart, becoming the highest-ranked K-pop album, ever, regardless of big-three affiliation or not. RM has said the album was inspired by the 1919 Jungian novel *Demian* by Hermann Hesse, a haughty literary reference for the boy band crowd. In one album version, he even recites from the text. As Amanda Petrusich summarized for the *New Yorker*, *Demian* is "a bildungsroman…in which a young boy named Emil Sinclair chooses self-realization over a world of illusions." I'd like to see the numbers on how many college freshmen declared liberal arts majors after its release.

Where most boy band lyrics, historically, are romance obsessed, BTS's now-embraced edge allowed them to tackle the topic with explicitly sexual undertones, as in their single "Blood Sweat & Tears" and its translated lyrics: "Kiss me, I don't care if it hurts / Hurry up and choke me / So I can't get hurt anymore / Baby, I don't care if I get drunk, I'll drink you / Deep into my throat, a whiskey called you." The subject matter resonated with American audiences, and in 2017, they performed it on *Jimmy Kimmel Live*.

That was the year BTS entered American consciousness in a way never before conceptualized by K-pop acts, the result of their willingness to do the work and continue to show face in the country when other acts did not. BTS performed at the American Music Awards, and they began their self-care-centric Love Yourself era, first with the EP comeback *Love Yourself: Her*, which sold

JIN

1.4 million physical copies worldwide by January 2018 and includes the manic single "DNA." Then came *Love Yourself: Tear* in spring 2018, featuring "Fake Love," and later, *Love Yourself: Answer*, with the bright "IDOL" and the grossly underappreciated Suga solo "Trivia: Seesaw." BTS began collaborating with Western pop acts like Steve Aoki, the Chainsmokers, Nicki Minaj, Halsey, and Ed Sheeran. They took home multiple Billboard Music Awards honors. They broke YouTube streaming records held by Taylor Swift. In 2019, they became the first K-pop artist to perform on *Saturday Night Live*. BTS clearly made it to the top. And their success has drawn more attention to the South Korean music business they came from.

FANTASTIC BABY: THE LEGACY OF BIG BANG

Before BTS there was another hip-hop boy band American media anticipated would one day rule the planet: YG's Big Bang, known as the Kings of K-pop. The band's plans were foiled by controversy (see the section titled "Sex, Drugs, Scandals, and Tragedies"), as well as lack of momentum following a brief hiatus and their *MADE* album series. Then, as if they needed a final nail to seal their career's already shuttered coffin, its members were forced into conscription. (In South Korea, men over eighteen are made to participate in compulsory military service for two years, regardless of their fame, fortune, or international notoriety.)

BTS owes much to the quintet—T.O.P, Taeyang, G-Dragon, Daesung, and Seungri were crucial in bringing K-pop to the United States. Not long after forming in 2006, Big Bang headlined

stadiums across North America before that would become the norm, when K-pop wasn't immediately accessible to curious listeners outside of Asia like it is today. They arrived at a crossroads in K-pop, a nebulous time between the music being something fans needed to seek out in order to participate in the fandom, and the monster business that it is now. You may remember a brief performance of their hit "Fantastic Baby" in season 4 of the hit show *Glee*.

Notwithstanding, Big Bang made strides. They collaborated with US artists like Diplo. They beat out Britney Spears to win Best Worldwide Act at the 2011 MTV Europe Music Awards. They were the source of much international press suggesting that they may become the first act post-Psy to really bring the K-pop phenomenon into the Western mainstream. That wasn't the case, but without Big Bang cracking the glass ceiling, BTS wouldn't have been able to smash it. In the immortal words of T.O.P: Boom-sha-ka-la-ka.

K-pop Glossary

K-POP REQUIRES its non-Korean-speaking fans to learn key phrases in the language, which is a really cool recent trend for an Anglo-centric entertainment business to learn from. English-speaking fans should be grateful that for so long, their language was industry standard.

The slang terms K-pop fans use vary from actual Korean expressions to internet colloquialisms unique to the culture, and therefore reading K-pop gossip online requires some translation. Take this glossary with you before diving into the Soompi archives. You'll need it.

4D: The eccentric personality of the group. Can be "weird" or playfully strange.

AEGYO: A display of cuteness, as in twee gesticulations. Example: forming a heart with your hands, resting your chin on your fingertips, etc.

AGE LINE: Idols (see below) born in the same year.

ANTI-FAN (OR ANTI): A hater.

ARMY: BTS's fandom name, an acronym for Adorable Representative M.C. for Youth.

BAGEL: A cute idol who happens to be ripped. If you manage to look away from his baby face, you'd notice you could grate cheese on his abs, etc.

BEAGLE: Idols who are both funny, loud, energetic, and hyper. When beagles go overboard with their unrivaled enthusiasms, they're labeled "kkab," which means essentially the same thing, just annoying and definitely not endearing.

BIAS: This is almost exactly what it sounds like. Your bias is the musician you adore, also known as your fave.

COMEBACK: The first song, track, music video, etc. from a new release. Not actually a reunion, but a new stage for the band.

DAEBAK: The Korean phrase for "big win" or "huge success"; can also be used as a synonym for "jackpot."

DONGSAENG: A familial term that means "younger sibling"; an endearing word used by elders to describe someone younger with whom they have a close relationship.

FAN CHANT: Self-explanatory: this is what fans chant at K-pop concerts. Sometimes they're specific to a song; sometimes it is the names of the members of the band in age order.

HALLYU: The Korean wave. Enthusiasms for all Korean culture, not only K-pop or Idol groups but also K-dramas, Korean food, etc. The term refers to the ever growing interest in South Korean culture from the 1990s onward.

HYUNG: A familial term that translates to "older brother."

IDOL: A K-pop star.

JJANG: Korean phrase for "that's the best!"

KCON: An annual convention in Los Angeles, New York City, and countries across the globe dedicated to "All Things Hallyu."

KILLING PART: The best part of a song.

KOREABOO: A non-Korean person who is obsessed with Korean culture. The term is taken from "Weeaboo," a word used to describe a non-Japanese person obsessed with Japanese culture. Both are often used derogatorily.

LEADER: The front man of a boy band…sometimes. This concept is unique to K-pop groups, since US, UK, and Australian boy bands refuse to designate one person as the leader. He's the member who usually speaks first publicly. More often than not, "leader" just means the oldest member of the group.

MAKNAE: The youngest member of a group. He's very cute.

NETIZEN: A portmanteau of "internet" and "citizen," a neologism for an avid 'net user (and because much of K-pop fandom happens online and in social media, those fans are netizens).

OPPA: The Korean word for "older brother," "big brother," or "strong older man," which K-pop fans sometimes use when talking about a member they have a crush on. Think of it like the K-pop version of "Daddy."

PERFECT ALL-KILL: When a release tops all eight of the major Korean music charts, Bugs, Genie, Melon, Mnet, Monkey3, Naver, Olleh, and Soribada, it's called a perfect all-kill.

SASAENG: Fans who won't stop at anything to get close to their idols; they often invade the privacy of the celebrity.

SATOORI: An accent or dialect.

SELCA: Korean for selfie.

SOOMPI: An English-language Korean culture news site—soon to be your new homepage.

SSANTI: A goofy dance.

SUB-UNIT: A smaller boy band built of members of a larger group, not unlike a side project.

TRAINEE: The stage before becoming an idol; varies in rigor and time.

VISUAL: The heartthrob of the boy band.

Style Watch

EACH ERA OF a K-pop group vastly differs from the one that preceded it, so naturally those ideas inform fashion. For boy bands like BTS, it means freedom from conformity. There's cohesion within the group, but they may play with color and style in a way that borders on the avant-garde. Unlike the Western groups touched upon in this book (with the exception of the Jonas Brothers' playfully ambisexual skintight pants, and twentysomething Harry Styles), K-pop disrupts traditional gender roles assigned to style. There are no limits to what those artists can do within that androgyny. Case in point: RM.

* RM changes the color of his hair a lot: black, icy blond, red, pastel blue, pink, brown, cool lavender, the list goes on and on, and dear Lord, how does it stay so soft? With the exception of 5 Seconds of Summer's Michael Clifford, whose hair was a mood ring in his band's pop-punk era, the perpetual hairstyle change is unusual within boy bands. Chopping a long mane to reveal slightly shorter hair is usually enough to make headlines and induce tears. Kudos to RM's follicles.

* Is this long coat a boudoir robe? Is it a seersucker cape, and is he ready for a yachting adventure with Dracula? (That last one should be a YA television series, and I await my royalty check.) The world may never know, but it is definitely unisex, and for that, props must be given.

* The leather pants return from the Backstreet Boys era, but this time, they're formfitting. Gotta love an idol who isn't afraid of a little chafing. Or does he douse his gams in baby powder before hitting the stage? Who among us hasn't been there?

* Shoes are all over the place for BTS, but slick black patent leather booties are a given. If there is a default fashionable shoe, it should be these. And with a heel, for the brazen.

METICULOUSLY COLORED HAIR
GENDERLESS BOUDOIR ROBE
RM
LEATHER SKINNIES
LEATHER BOOTIES I'D LOVE TO BORROW

Sex, Drugs, Scandals, and Tragedies

THE EXPECTATION FOR a K-pop artist to be controversy-free far exceeds those limitations placed on Western acts, which could speak to traditionalism in South Korea. To quote Tiffany Young of K-pop girl group Girls' Generation, who grew up in California and moved to Seoul for her music, "I thought I would be able to adjust, because my parents spoke Korean at home, but I didn't even imagine how different it would be. American culture is so open compared to Korean culture, which is really conservative. So I would be, like, 'Hi!' and they were, like, 'You don't say "Hi!" You bow!'"

For Korean boy bands to appear accessible to a fan base of all ages, there can be no scandals with women or men, no drugs of any kind (even the ones that aren't so bad), no excessive booze consumption, and no draft dodging, which, of course, is straight-up illegal. The punishment for each vary in scope, but there is one consistency: scandals dominate K-pop gossip head-lines. Like all taboo topics, these range from minor offenses to life-shattering and sometimes life-ending issues that shouldn't be taken lightheartedly.

Sex

As they are in all countries, sex crimes are a cultural issue in South Korea that have grown to fester. There's even a Korean word specifically for the act of filming someone without their permission, otherwise known as hidden camera porn: *molka*. Sex crime allegations invaded the K-pop boy band sphere in early 2019, when Big Bang's *maknae*, Seungri, was booked as a suspect in relation to allegations of supplying investors with "drug addled" prostitutes at a nightclub in Seoul. Seungri denied the charges and immediately announced his retirement from the music business on Instagram. "As this scandal is too big, I have decided to retire," he wrote, translation via the *Guardian*. "As for the ongoing investigation, I will take it seriously to clear myself of all the allegations." At the time of writing this, there has yet to be a conviction. The investigation continues.

When the Seungri accusations were first publicized, YG saw their stock prices fall sharply, and Seo Taiji and Boys' Yang "Goon" Hyun-suk, YG's founder, stepped down from his position not long afterward. When alleged crimes like these become public record in the West, accused artists often see a spike in streams and sales, the total moral opposite. After the 2019 Lifetime docuseries *Surviving R. Kelly* outlined dozens of allegations of sexual abuse at the hands of the R&B singer, which he denied, Kelly saw an increase of Spotify streams of 16 percent. When rapper XXXTentacion died while awaiting trial on felony charges of domestic violence and imprisonment of his pregnant girlfriend, his streams climbed 549 percent. Their careers were bolstered by their disturbing allegations. In K-pop, a musical world often viewed publicly as virtuous and clean-cut, purported injustices have consequences.

Drugs

Unlike more forgiving Western markets, where getting zooted on ganja isn't chastised but commended (examples: hip-hop and stoner metal), offenses like smoking weed can hinder or halt a K-pop career. When Big Bang's G-Dragon gave a weak positive for marijuana consumption in 2011, for example, he disappeared from public eye for the better part of two months. Even though South Korea is militant with its anti-weed laws, the amount was slight, and he was released without indictment. It's hard to imagine the same sort of castigation happening to a US singer who lights one up. His band mate T.O.P., too, received a ten-month suspended sentence for smoking weed "several times" in 2017. In other words: all of your white friends from high school would be in prison right now.

Mental Health

I'm going to give it to you straight: mental health is a verboten subject for a lot of people. Around the globe, perpetually exhausted boy bands are often allowed to express feelings of anxiety and depression publicly as long as they stop short of a diagnosis or any language that goes beyond the guise of relatability and vulnerability. There have been some strides in shedding the stigma, but the derogation endures in South Korea, as it does everywhere else. In 2010, Lee Joon of the popular K-pop boy band MBLAQ revealed he was diagnosed with bipolar disorder. It was a groundbreaking revelation at the time, taking into account the country's prevailing denial of those illnesses.

Suicidal ideation and attempts are a clear and present danger: the industry was rocked in 2017 when Kim Jong-hyun (stage name Jonghyun), a singer in the boy band SHINee, died by suicide. He left a note in his Cheongdam-dong apartment outlining the dangerous effects of fame on mental health. South Korea has one of the highest suicide rates in the developed world, a number that has continued to increase since the 1990s. Clearly, something needs to change, and K-pop fans might help in leading the way. After Jonghyun's tragic passing, fans shared their own mental health journeys in an attempt to get rid of the taboo surrounding open and honest conversation, the kind crucial to healing. No wonder one of the biggest K-pop boy bands of all time is BTS, a group unafraid to tackle these hard-to-swallow themes, especially as they affect young people. As Suga told *Billboard* in 2018, "I really want to say that everyone in the world is lonely and everyone is sad, and if we know that everyone is suffering and lonely, I hope we can create an environment where we can ask for help, and say things are hard when they're hard."

CHAPTER NINE

LET'S ALL MEET UP IN THE YEAR 3000: THE FUTURE OF BOY BANDS

PICTURE A WORLD inspired by the Busted classic made famous by the Jonas Brothers, "Year 3000." It's a fully realized future that, in the song's lyrics, promise "Boy bands / And another one / And another one / And another one." It's a new millennium. Time machines exist and somehow operate while submerged in water. Women have three breasts now, and they hang around town in the nude, I assume because only pop stars and women have survived whatever horrific climate change disaster has turned Earth into a giant Atlantis. Other than that, everything is pretty much the same. Even in this totally decent dystopic utopia, there's only one consistency throughout

Busted's lyrical prophecy: each generation continues to get the boy band they deserve.[*]

Points should be awarded to the band for creativity and for that final accuracy: as you've encountered in this book, interest in boy bands is a trend that does come and go, with "another one, and another one, and another one" ready to take the place of the one that preceded it. Fans grow disinterested with the groups of their adolescence and only confront them in care packages from their moms or in a rare moment of nostalgic vulnerability. (Why did she send you that old boy band T-shirt, again? The acne wipes were a nice touch.) At the time of this writing in 2019, the world is in the midst of K-pop dominion with seemingly no end in sight. Seoul sounds reign supreme and offer something that has never been seen before: a musical entertainment engine outside of the United States, England, or Australia shaping the future of teen pop music, the prosperity of which has only just begun. The planet is not yet underwater. What comes next cannot be predicted.

Copycat bands have begun cropping up in K-pop, both in and outside South Korea. In New York, EXP Edition, a "K-pop" group of non-Koreans, formed as the result of a Columbia University student's project. The validity of their group is up for the consumer to decide. Could it be that the future of Western pop music mimics the Eastern pop music that was founded on Western pop music? Is this yet another extension of the boy

---

[*] It also appears that in the year 3000, gender-based discrimination has been eliminated, so that those who identify as women can move about the planet naked and free, without fear of harm. Talk about an added benefit. Sign me up.

band trend widening into some unknowable panopticon, where fans are thrust in the middle? Are all fans cogs in some beautiful boy band machine? Have you tried reading this paragraph backward, to see if it spells out some secret message, effectively answering all of these questions with Nostradamus-like psychic precision unlike your horoscope this morning? (It doesn't. Don't try it. I'm not clever enough for covert messages. Blame Mercury in retrograde.)

It's too early to tell. In my opinion, labeling a group like EXP Edition as "K-pop" is problematic. They studied in Seoul and perform bilingual hits, but without the formal trainee process, affiliating with an entertainment agency in the country, or actually having a Korean member, are they really part of it? Western boy bands have been pushing the envelope in other ways in an attempt to become the next great movement. Most notably, they've ditched the sugary-sweet antics and adopted the too-cool-for-school-but-cute swagger that made BTS the biggest boy band on the planet. Boy bands can be disruptive, according to these newer acts, and they can embrace the boy band label, too, unlike, say, One Direction's Zayn Malik, who announced in the 2013 film *One Direction: This Is Us*, "When people say you're in a boy band, I'm like, *yeah*, I am, but a cool boy band." He agreed to the term, but begrudgingly. The modern acts that have cropped up in the last few years may be in their infancy, but they also argue against the qualifier of "cool," lessening the cultural smirching of boy bands. They're in a boy band, a cool boy band, because being in a boy band is cool. Maybe that is what Busted predicted all along.

Let's look at a few of those groups, because it is about damn time boy bands own up to being boy bands.

CNCO

In 2016, Simon Cowell and Ricky Martin joined forces to create *La Banda*, a Spanish-language singing reality TV show on Univision. The winners of its first season, Erick Brian Colón, Christopher Vélez Muñoz, Zabdiel De Jesús, Richard Camacho, and Joel Pimentel, were brought together in the show's finale and named CNCO, pronounced C-N-C-O, and taken from the Spanish word for five, "*cinco*," reflective of the group's five-member base. (5ive was not available for comment.) They won a five-year recording contract with Sony Latin, essentially the same kind of contract One Direction signed, and their reggaeton-heavy debut album featured rapper Wisin. They are one of Cowell's post–One Direction boy bands, meant to fill the great need for Latino groups. Now that popular culture is more open to crossover acts than ever before, it could be their time to shine. My kingdom for a Bad Bunny collab.

IN REAL LIFE

With a name perfect for the social media age, In Real Life formed on the 2017 ABC reality television show *Boy Band*, which, judging by its cancelation after one season, I was the only one who watched. Unlike past American boy bands, these five gents—Brady Tutton, Chance Perez, Drew Ramos, Sergio Calderon, and Michael Conor—possess a rapper and a Latino heartthrob (that shouldn't be deemed noteworthy, but this is our reality; most of the biggest boy bands in the West, and all of their heartthrobs, have been white). After winning the show, the quintet signed with Hollywood Records and opened for the 2018 American Idol tour.

WHY DON'T WE

Why Don't We is a viral success story. The group—Jack Avery, Corbyn Besson, Zach Herron, Daniel Seavey (who appeared on season 14 of *American Idol*), and Jonah Marais, who previously toured with celebrities from the defunct six-second video sharing platform Vine like Cameron Dallas and Nash Grier—first got together in 2016, but were massively popular before then, garnering a following for appearing in YouTube videos alongside unruly personality Logan Paul. (You know Paul as the twenty-something who got in trouble for filming a corpse in the Aokigahara Suicide Forest at the foot of Japan's Mount Fuji in 2018. He's not a great guy to associate with.) Most of Why Don't We's music deals directly with teen angst, dating itself with references to trust-fund babies, Instagram thotties, and not fitting in at the club. But hey, what do I know, I'm old.

BROCKHAMPTON

If there is a popular American group tasked with the title of "cutting-edge boy band," it's the San Marcos, Texas, double-digit musical collective Brockhampton. They were founded in 2010 following the vision of front person Kevin Abstract, who posted a call for members on the hip-hop blog Kanye To The. After a name change from AliveSinceForever and enough time post–high school to figure out what this thing was meant to be, Abstract rebranded the band. In 2017, Brockhampton became the subject of a Vice show called *American Boyband*, principally because the group has referred to themselves as one since their inception. The question is now, does calling yourself a boy band actually make you one? Based on the theory presented in chapter 2, no way. Their shows are comfortably mixed-gender instead of appealing primarily to young women, among other factors. But if boy bands actually do come in all shapes and sizes and continue to modify with contemporary culture, does that matter? BTS, for goodness' sake, was founded in gangster rap. Why can't Brockhampton be the first hip-hop boy band collective? One that genuinely appeals to straight dudes as well?

PRETTYMUCH

PrettyMuch, the adorable quintet of Brandon Arreaga, Edwin Honoret, Austin Porter, Nick Mara, and Zion Kuwonu, was created by Simon Cowell in 2016. (You could say they've got their eyes set in…One Direction. I do. A lot.) Unlike 1D, the fivesome can dance and love to dance instead of simply harmonizing like angels and flopping around onstage. PrettyMuch's approach to the boy band role is less pop-rock and more R&B-pop. Their debut single, "Would You Mind," dropped in September 2017 and peaked at number 40 on the Billboard Pop Songs chart, nothing to scoff at for a band plucked from relative obscurity. And get this: the song was co-written by Savan Kotecha, the same Max Martin–adjacent genius who gave One Direction their career-making single, "What Makes You Beautiful." If Cowell's done it before, who says he can't do it again?

R5

With all the boy bands and girl groups in popular music history, there really hasn't been a successful co-ed ensemble that fits the formula. Once genders are mixed, the dynamic is altered, and the project simply becomes "a band." Family bands of a variety of genders haven't really flown since the '70s, but Hollywood Records' R5 might've been the first in a long, unfruitful lineage to flip the script. Like the Jackson 5 five decades prior, R5 was built of five siblings: lead vocalist/guitarist Ross Lynch, bassist Riker Lynch, guitarist Rocky Lynch, keyboardist Rydel Lynch (who happens to be a woman), and Rydel's partner, drummer Ellington Ratliff. Their live shows inspired the same sort of audience as boy band shows—overwhelmingly young and female, their cumulative scream deafening everyone within a one-mile radius—but with the inclusion of Rydel, they could never really be called a "boy band." In 2018, the group rebranded as a duo, the Driver Era, consisting only of Ross and Rocky, so it looks like the world will never know what could've been. Who's to say that in the future a boy band must only be made of boys?

KING CALAWAY

Historically, boy bands don't venture too far into unfamiliar musical territory. They keep their interest pop- and R&B-focused. (Any traversing into hip-hop and EDM is a direct reflection of what's on the radio. Think of the Jonas Brothers as a good example: in the mid-'00s, their pop-punk-rock was similar enough to what was happening on *TRL*, but different enough for young fans to claim as their own.) That said, it was only a matter of time before other musical styles went the boy band route, and King Calaway is country music's first manufactured boy band (excluding AJ McLean's middle-aged foray into the genre). The group, made up of Caleb Miller, Chris Deaton, Gibraltar's Simon Dumas, Scotland's Jordan Harvey, Chad Michael Jervis, and Austin Luther, formed in Nashville in 2018 as a country-pop take on what one of their music directors refers to as "the Eagles meets One Direction." Judging by their successes, including *American Idol* golden tickets and performances at the famed Grand Ole Opry, combined with popular culture's interest in all things yeehaw, it wouldn't be surprising to see more and more country idols materializing, even if country music purists aren't in favor.

NO DAUGHTER OF MINE

In 2018, four twenty-somethings—Ethan Remillard, Xander Idris, Rowan Seitz, and Cole Hayes—launched and fully funded a Seed and Spark crowdfunding page for *Born Stars*, a web series documenting their journey to becoming a boy band. Sounds inconsequential enough, except that all four men are trans and are working on the project with a fully LGBTQIA+ crew, which Hayes has described as crucial because, "Trans visibility…transmasculine visibility, is very limited." He's not wrong. The group originally took on the name Ladyboy but changed it to No Daughter of Mine to reappropriate language weaponized against the trans community. A boy band built of trans boys has never happened before, and it furthers expressions of boy band masculinity, bringing it into unchartered territory. Who will be their audience? Will they market themselves to a tween and teen audience, as most apolitical cis boy bands have done? Will they play into the same archetypes and platitudes? Or is this something different entirely?

AN EDUCATED GUESS

If the way pop culture dissects gender progresses into more tolerant territory, and the world miraculously survives a few more decades with humanity somehow aboard, newly empathetic for one another after having to come together to salvage our biosphere, boy bands will continue to exist free of the condescension of straight older brothers everywhere. Or not, because there will be no boys, only fleshy bodies and brains and voices to fall in love with. In reality, with the way things are headed, future boy bands will probably be built entirely of artificial intelligence, performing songs that require individual approval by Supreme Dictator Elon Musk, or Jeff Bezos, who acquired ruling power in a bloody coup. Music can be a powerful tool for oppression as much as it frees us.

Apocalyptic jokes aside, I will say this: many of the boy bands discussed in this book come from working-class families. Their success and wealth became aspirational not only to their fans, but also to their communities. Their triumphs suggest that with a little hard work, elbow grease, and passion for the task at hand, you can accomplish anything. That might be the foundational tenet of the American Dream, but it's also not honest: these musicians are guys privileged with luck, talent, external support, and conventionally attractive faces. If anything, there are lessons to be learned from boy band fans themselves: the ones who shout, unabashedly, about their pleasurable pop music passions; those who use their encyclopedic knowledge to excel in creative endeavors in and

outside of the entertainment umbrella (as the great critic Jessica Hopper once proposed, replace the word "fangirl" with "expert" and see what happens), and those who allow boy band music to enter their lives and fill them with joy. Boy bands throughout the decades have always found a way to be intentionally vague and purposeful in their "no matter what you're going through, we're here for you" messaging so we, the fans, could assign meaning to them, not the other way around. We've always had the power to write the narrative. And isn't that magical?

The next time you're DIYing an "I love Donnie" T-shirt with puffy paint and glitter purchased at your favorite craft store (Jo-Ann's hive, assemble) to prepare for the upcoming New Kids on the Block cruise with your friends from high school, or digging through your old Beatles magazine clippings, or pressing play on that godforsaken O-Town Hit Clip that miraculously works, or revisiting your illegally pirated CD copy of *Millennium* or Aventura's *We Broke the Rules*, or singing "Best Song Ever" in a seedy karaoke bar downtown, or buying a $60 globe-shaped light stick at a BTS stadium concert, take a moment to remember that while every generation gets their own boy band, you are responsible for making yours what they were and they can continue to be, for so many.

And that makes you larger than life.

ACKNOWLEDGMENTS

Don't bore us, get to the chorus: I want to thank everyone who has ever supported me. As Harry and Liam harmonize in "Don't Forget Where You Belong," I feel like I'm dreaming.

This one is for Mom and Dad and Erik, thank you for emboldening me to never question my ambitions, even when it became immediately apparent that I didn't possess any conventional talent.

This book would've never happened if my brilliant editor Lisa Tenaglia didn't cold email me to ask if I've ever considered authoring a text on this particular passion. Her guidance made the process as painless as possible, and I'm so grateful for her patience and expertise. That sentiment extends to all of the Black Dog and Leventhal/Hachette dream team: Kara Thornton, Melanie Gold, Katie Benezra, and Betsy Hulsebosch, my hat goes off to you. Alex Fine, thank you for making this fanatical text a gorgeous art object people will actually want to own and keep in their home. I apologize for giving notes like, "Can we define his cavernous dimples a bit more?" Carolyn Schurr Levin, thank you for schooling me on the American One Direction. Lori Paximadis, I will never look at an em dash the same way again.

To my heroes who became friends, without whom I would have no career to speak of, this one's also for you: Rob Sheffield, Amanda Petrusich, Steve Kandell, Ann Powers, Jessica Hopper, Lars Gotrich, Anna Bond, and Maura Johnston. I hope to make you proud. To my friends who became heroes, without whom I would have no interesting observations on boy bands to speak of, you are the girls almighty: Brittany Spanos, Brodie Lancaster, Marissa Lorusso, Jenny Gathright, Allyson Gross, and Erin Browne.

Thanks to Jon Caramanica for allowing me to use the *New York Times'* Popcast to announce this book to the world and to Tamar Herman, the most brilliant K-pop journalist going, for fact-checking me out of the kindness of her heart (and the promise of karaoke, I assume). Thanks to Mike Ayers, for making sure I knew what questions to ask; to Annie Zaleski, for introducing me to the Authors Guild, who made sure I knew how to ask the questions I was supposed to ask; and to Derek James, for reminding me of every Jonas Brothers factoid in excruciating detail.

All my gratitude to the friends that I couldn't have made it through without and the colleagues who took a chance on me (and those who fit into both categories): Hannah Silk Champagne, the best human and soup enthusiast the world has ever seen, Tori Cote, Shaun Sutkus, Ben Bondy, Chloe Hutton, and Michael Laviolette for still wanting to hang out with me, Tori Hardy, Jatnna Nuñez, David Glickman, Rogelio Hernandez, Jes Skolnik, Suzy Exposito, Paula Mejia, Zachary Lipez, Jill Mapes, Jason Pettigrew, Kip Berman, Geoff Rickly, Ilana Kaplan, Ryan Leas, Jon Blistein, Matthew Ruiz, Charlotte Zoller, Mitchell Wojcik, Michael Tedder, Ric Leichtung, Brenna Ehrlich, J. Edward Keyes, Zoe Camp, Harris Penn, Ying Lam, Elia Einhorn, John Norris, and Josh Madden and the Good Charlotte family. My editors and employers, past and future. Everyone in Philly. Everyone in NYC. Everyone in LA. Everyone in Austin. Everyone in Toronto. Everyone else I've failed to mention here. Twee bands and hardcore punks. Puerto Rico. WNYU and everyone I met through college radio. If you are reading this while in college, join your college radio station.

To Matt Ern, my first love, don't make me regret thanking you here when I'm 80.

And most of all, I'd like to thank you—the reader—for spending some time with this book. Bonus points will be awarded if you actually enjoyed it. As the most romantic song in the universe goes: I do, cherish you, for the rest of my life.

RECOMMENDED READING

No book exists without the texts that came before it, and this book is no exception. *Larger Than Life* would've never been possible without those brilliant musicians, thinkers, critics, journalists, and academics who saw real merit in the boy band story long before I was old enough to know what Jodeci songs were really about. For that reason, here's a short selection of titles that made this project a reality. Consider it your extra-credit reading. I'm the professor and, judging by the fifty-page bibliography I tried to submit to my publisher, you're getting off easy.

Lance Bass's *Out of Sync*

Hannah Ewens's *Fangirls: Scenes from Modern Music Culture*

Nelson George's *Where Did Our Love Go? The Rise and Fall of the Motown Sound*

Tyler Gray's *The Hit Charade: Lou Pearlman, Boy Bands, and the Biggest Ponzi Scheme in U.S. History*

Georgina Gregory's *Boy Bands and the Performance of Pop Masculinity*

Euny Hong's *The Birth of Korean Cool: How One Nation Is Conquering the World Through Pop Culture*

Steve Knopper's *Appetite for Self-Destruction: The Spectacular Crash of the Record Industry in the Digital Age*

Frederick Levy's *The Ultimate Boy Band Book*

Nikki Van Noy's *New Kids on the Block: Five Brothers and a Million Sisters, the Authorized Biography*

Rob Sheffield's *Talking to Girls About Duran Duran: One Young Man's Quest for True Love and a Cooler Haircut*

Caroline Sullivan's *Bye Bye Baby: My Tragic Love Affair with the Bay City Rollers*

INDEX